THE
BEATLES
LIVERPOOL

Ron Jones

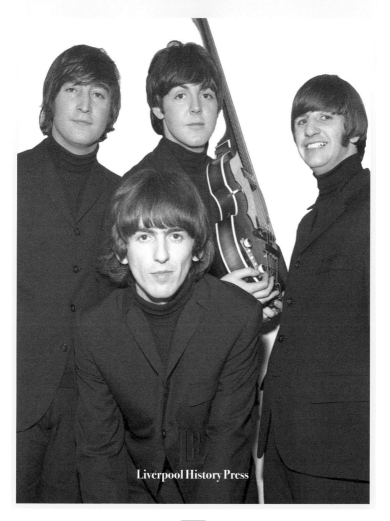

Liverpool History Press

Liverpool History Press

www.liverpoolhistorypress.co.uk

This book is dedicated to the memory of my parents
Charles and Frances Jones

Reprinted 2017 & 2018 (twice, with minor amendments)

This Liverpool History Press edition published 2016.

First published in Great Britain in 1991 by Ron Jones Associates.

ISBN: 978-0-9573833-5-7

Written and designed by Ron Jones.

Published by the Liverpool History Press (a Ron Jones imprint).

Email: ron@rja-mpl.com

www.liverpoolhistorypress.co.uk

Printed and bound in the U.K.

FOR LIVERPOOL ...
BIRTHPLACE OF THE BEATLES

There are places I'll remember all my life,
Though some have changed,
Some forever, not for better,
Some have gone and some remain.

All these places had their moments,
With lovers and friends I still can recall,
Some are dead and some are living,
In my life I've loved them all.

In My Life by John Lennon and Paul McCartney.

LIDDYPOOL ('Liverpool' by John Lennon)

This visitor's guide to 'Liddypool' (Liverpool) by John Lennon was published in his book *In His Own Write*, although it first appeared in the *Mersey Beat* newspaper:

"Reviving the old tradition of Judro Bathing is slowly but slowly dancing in Liddypool once more. Had you remembering these owld custard of Boldy Street blowing? The Peer Hat is very popularce for sun eating and Boots for Nude Brighter is handys when sailing. We are not happy with Queen Victorious Monologue, but Walky Through Gallery is goodly when the rain and Sit Georgie House is black (and white from the little pilgrims flying from Hellsy College). Talk Hall is very histerical with old things wot are fakes and King Anne never slept there I tell you. Shout Airborne is handly for planes if you like (no longer government patrolled) and the L.C.C.C. (Liddypool Cha Cha Cha) are doing a great thing. The Mersey Boat is selling another three copies to some go home foreigners who went home.

There is a lot to do in Liddypool, but not all convenience."

But what does it all mean? As Paul McCartney said in the introduction to John's book... "None of it has to make sense, and if it seems funny then that's enough."

Here's my interpretation although I haven't a clue what his first sentence means!

Can you remember the old custom of Bold Street blowing? The Pier Head is very popular for sun bathing and boats are handy for sailing to New Brighton. We are not happy with the Queen Victoria Monument, but the Walker Art Gallery is good when it's raining and St George's Hall is black (and white from the little pigeons). Speke Hall is very historical with old things that are fakes and I can tell you that Queen Anne never slept there. Speke Airport is handy if you like planes (it's no longer government controlled) and Liverpool City Council are doing a great job. The 'Mersey Beat' is selling another three copies to some "Go home foreigners!" who went home.

There is a lot to do in Liverpool, but not all of it is convenient.

John: *"Who knows why The Beatles happened? It's like the constant search for why you go down one road or why you go down another. It has as much to do with being from Liverpool, or being from Quarry Bank grammar school or being in a household where the library was full of Oscar Wilde and Whistler and Fitzgerald and all the Book of the Month Club."*

Yoko Ono: *"...this is Liverpool. It is my husband John's birthplace and the place that he never stopped talking about all his life".*

CONTENTS

BIRTHPLACE OF THE BEATLES

As I remember it: The year is 1961. The Cuban heels of your winklepicker shoes clack noisily on the wet cobblestones. You turn up the collar on your short 'bum freezer' jacket to keep out the cold November wind that whips through this narrow canyon of a street flanked by age-blackened warehouses.

Light, and sound, spill from an open doorway. You head towards it. Excitement grips your stomach. You edge past the bulky frame of doorman Paddy Delaney who nods approval at the membership card held up for inspection. Carefully, for they are worn and steep, you descend, with quickening heartbeat, the eighteen stone steps into the blackness below.

As you reach the bottom, it hits you like a sledgehammer. The wall of heat given off by a multitude of perspiring bodies. That odour, a mixture of cheap disinfectant, sweat, cigarette smoke and the mustiness of ancient cellars. The catacomb darkness pierced by a few naked light bulbs.

And the sound. Especially the sound. That all-consuming sound that sears the brain. The driving rhythm hacked out on the Rickenbacker, the melody robustly overlaid by the Gretsch. Underpinning it, the booming Hofner violin bass and, binding it all together, the unrelenting beat punched out on the drums.

You elbow a pathway through to the centre of the three aisles and look over the sea of bobbing heads, willing your eyes to cut through the fug to see who is producing that unique, exciting sound. As if confirmation were necessary. It could only come from one source.

Four figures clad in worn black leathers and sweat-sodden tee-shirts dominate the tiny wooden stage which threatens to shatter beneath the sheer power of the beat that is their hallmark. All eyes are fixed on the lead singer. Legs apart, hunched over his Rickenbacker, the microphone is but a whisper away from his lips. Through tortured vocal cords comes a raw sound which, despite the inferno-like heat, causes you to shiver... "You make me dizzy Miss Lizzy, with your rock and roll..."

Yes. This is the Cavern, Mathew Street. On stage is the greatest rock and roll band the world has ever known...the Beatles!

And this is Liverpool, 'City of the Beatles': We love you – Yeah! Yeah! Yeah!

Ron Jones

Pier Head, Liverpool 1961.

WALKING IN THE FOOTSTEPS OF THE BEATLES IN LIVERPOOL CITY CENTRE

The pages that follow set out a grand Liverpool City Centre Beatles trail. All of the important Beatle places and most of the tourist sights in the City Centre are included on this walk. Some stops on the trail either no longer exist in the form they did in 1950s and 60s or have changed their appearance but you can satisfy yourself that, wherever you walk on this trail, you will be 'walking in the footsteps of the Beatles'. And, of course, you can simply 'imagine' how things were more than half a century ago. Coincidentally, the trail takes you through parts of the historic waterfront and city centre which were designated by UNESCO as a World Heritage Site in 2004. In 2015 UNESCO also honoured Liverpool by naming it as a 'City of Music', one of only ten such cities in the world named that year and the only one in England.

Not allowing for any stops, it should take you about two hours to follow this trail. I suggest that you start at the Albert Dock where there are parking facilities, toilets and lots of eating and drinking places. Added to that it's Liverpool's top visitor attraction, home to the Beatles Story and a starting point for the Magical Mystery Bus Tour (see p10). The trail starts at the Beatles Story and ends in Mathew Street (see p46). If it's more convenient, you could start there and finish at Albert Dock – simply follow the trail in reverse order.

As an aid for finding your way around when you are in Liverpool, and to make it easier to locate the various places on your devices, the postcode has been added to each of the locations on the trails. Simply put the word 'Liverpool' and the postcode in Google maps and you will be able to view the location on a map. And, by using the map's Google Street View (just drag the little yellow man to the nearest road), you will be able to explore the location and surrounding area 'for real'. Cool!

Don't forget your camera; there are lots of interesting Beatle landmarks and, as an added bonus, Liverpool is an incredibly photogenic city.

HELP!

Please respect the privacy of the people who live in the houses mentioned in these Beatles trails. Don't disturb them by knocking on their doors, peeping through their windows or otherwise trespassing on their property. The Beatles left Liverpool long ago and none of their families now live in any of these houses.

Liverpool City Centre

Mersey Ferry, Pier Head and Liverpool Waterfront 2016.

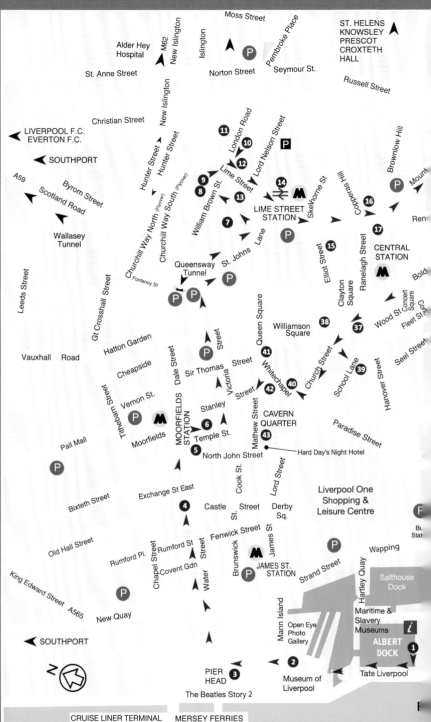

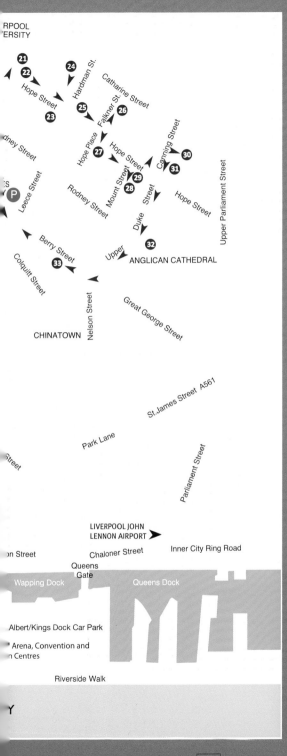

1. Albert Dock/Beatles Story
2. Museum of Liverpool
3. Mersey Ferry/Beatles Story/ Beatles Statue
4. Liverpool Town Hall
5. Former Cassanova Club 1
6. Former Iron Door Club
7. St John's Gardens
8. Picton Library
9. Walker Art Gallery
10. Former Odeon Cinema
11. Former Cassanova Club 2
12. Empire Theatre
13. St George's Hall
14. Lime Street Train Station
15. Former Blacklers Store
16. Adelphi Hotel
17. Former Lewis's Store
18. 64 Mount Pleasant
19. 4 Rodney Street
20. R.C. Cathedral
21. Former Maternity Hospital
22. Everyman Theatre
23. Philharmonic Pub
24. Former Children's Hospital
25. Philharmonic Hall
26. 36 Falkner Street
27. Ye Cracke Pub
28. Former Liverpool Institute
29. Former College of Art
30. 7 Percy Street
31. 3 Gambier Terrace
32. Liverpool Cathedral
33. Blue Angel Club
34. Former Mersey Beat Office
35. Bold Street
36. Jacaranda
37. Epstein Theatre
38. Former Reece's Restaurant
39. Bluecoat Chambers
40. Former NEMS
41. Former Rushworth's Music
42. Former Hessy's Music Store
43. Cavern Quarter: see pages 45-51

STARTING POINT: THE BEATLES STORY / ALBERT DOCK *(L3 4AD)*

Liverpool City Centre

No visitor to Liverpool should leave the city without visiting the Albert Dock, and not just because it is home to The Beatles Story, the city's one and only Beatles 'museum'. The converted warehouses, dating from 1846, form the largest group of Grade One 'listed' buildings (on account of their historical and architectural importance) in Britain. The complex, a mixture of world-class museums and galleries, shops, restaurants and bars, hotels, luxury apartments and offices, is the most popular free heritage attraction in the country, pulling in some six million visitors a year. The Albert Dock is also the departure point for the **Magical Mystery Tour** bus which operates daily from 11am: the Ticket Office is in Anchor Courtyard.

In the basement of Britannia Pavilion is **The Beatles Story**, the brainchild of Mike and Bernie Byrne, which opened in 1990. The Beatles Story is literally that...the story of the Beatles from their childhood days through to their break-up and the pursuit of individual careers. This is done by way of a series of rooms including the office of the Mersey Beat newspaper, Hamburg's Reeperbahn, the Cavern and Mathew Street, the Casbah Coffee Club, the Yellow Submarine, a Lennon 'White Room' etc.

An extension, opened in 2008, effectively doubled the size of The Beatles Story. The gallery, *Going Solo,* focuses on the individual Beatles' solo careers and a special exhibition space stages a changing programme of themed exhibitions. A hands-on,

inter-active Discovery Zone will be of special interest to families and school groups. Creature comforts are catered for in the Starbucks Café and chill-out area whilst a large Fab4Store completes the visitor experience.

To get the most out of your visit, opt for the "Living History" tour, narrated by John Lennon's half-sister Julia. You'll also hear the voices of Brian Epstein, Paul McCartney, Allan Williams, Cynthia Lennon and George Martin as they tell you about the group's rise to fame. The tour is available in ten languages. For the latest information, booking admission tickets on-line, browsing the on-line shop etc., check out - *www.beatlesstory.com*

The Beatles Story is owned by Merseytravel which also operates a Beatles satellite attraction nearby at the Mersey Ferries terminal, Pier Head (see p13).

To the immediate right of The Beatles Story is the main entrance to Albert Dock. Turn left onto the quayside and follow it round past **Tate Liverpool**. There are no Beatles connections as such but, if you have the time and modern art is your thing, it's worth a visit. Café and toilets.

Liverpool City Centre

Across the Hartley Bridge, to the right, is the **Merseyside Maritime Museum** which incorporates the **International Slavery Museum** both of which should be on your 'must visit' list, as should the **Museum of Liverpool** – it's the strikingly modern white building straight ahead of you; head for the *Wondrous Place* gallery on the top floor where you will find a special Beatles display of memorabilia (pictured right), including stage suits worn by the Fab Four, a jacket that belonged to ousted Beatle, Pete Best, and a re-creation of John and Yoko's 1969 Amsterdam 'bed-in' stunt.

There's also a short audio-visual Beatles Show in a small theatre which boasts the actual stage from St Peter's Church Hall where John and Paul met and played together for the very first time on 6 July 1957 – see p75.

Admission to all three museums is free. This is true for all seven museums and galleries under the control of National Museums Liverpool.

Before it was redeveloped, the Kings Dock area, immediately south of the Albert Dock, was the setting for a fabulous *Let It Be Liverpool* open air concert staged by Paul on the evening of 28th June 1990. He was back again on 1st June 2003 to perform the final gig of his world tour. The area is now home to the new Liverpool Exhibition Centre and Liverpool Echo Arena / BT Convention Centre. The latter opened on 12 January 2008 with Ringo and a host of other local musical luminaries taking part in the opening event – *Liverpool - The Musical*. Paul also played a gig there on 20 December 2011, shortly after his marriage to American heiress Nancy Shevell, and another one on 28 May 2015.

(Leave Albert Dock by crossing the footbridge over the entrance to the dock and head towards the Museum of Liverpool and the Pier Head.)

THE PIER HEAD: BEATLES STATUE / MERSEY FERRIES / THE BEATLES STORY *(L3 1DP)*

Departure point for the famous Mersey Ferries and cruise liners. The Pier Head and its landmark Edwardian era buildings: the Cunard Building, Port of Liverpool Building, and especially the Royal Liver Building topped by the mythical twin Liver Birds, are powerful emotive symbols of the city for all *Liverpudlians*, *Scousers* or *Wackers,* as we are variously called.

It has always been an especially favourite place for Liverpool children and the Beatles were no exception. They would be drawn here to marvel at the giant transatlantic liners which were such a glamorous feature of the Pier Head until the early 1970s. A cruise liner terminal, opened in 2007, has seen increasing numbers of cruise-ships including Liverpool in their itineraries. No doubt the Beatles also rode on the now-demolished Overhead Electric Railway, the world's first, and nick-named *The Docker's Umbrella*, which gave them a bird's eye view of the then booming Liverpool docks stretching from Dingle in the south, near Ringo's home, to Seaforth in the north.

John, Paul, George and Ringo would travel here on bone-rattling *Green Goddesses*, Liverpool's much-missed electric trams, pensioned off in 1957. Here they'd catch the ferryboats that would take them across the fast-flowing River Mersey to the funfair and sands at New Brighton or the beaches at Wallasey.

It is therefore fitting that the city's newest Beatles attraction is to be found here – a larger-than-lifesize **Beatles statue**. Crafted by sculptor Andy Edwards, the 1.2 ton artwork was commissioned by Cavern City Tours (owners of the Cavern Club) who generously met the reported cost of £200,000 and gifted it to the City of Liverpool. It was unveiled on 4 December 2015 by John Lennon's half-sister, Julia Baird, almost 50 years to the day that the Beatles gave their final public performance in Liverpool at the Empire Theatre. The statue, which depicts the Beatles simply 'walking along a street in 1963', proved an instant hit with visitors who line up to take 'selfies' or have their photograph taken in front of those 'Four Lads from Liverpool' and against the iconic backdrop of the city's 'Big Three' waterfront buildings.

A sight that would have been familiar to all four Beatles in the 1950s: the Royal Iris returns to the Pier Head from a trip to New Brighton. A Canadian Pacific liner and a Cunarder are berthed at the Princes Landing Stage.

The ferry to New Brighton has long gone but you can still savour one of the truly essential Liverpool experiences – a trip on one of the famous old **Mersey Ferries**, built at the beginning of the 1960s. These Merseybeat-era ferries are immortalised in the Gerry and the Pacemakers song *Ferry 'cross the Mersey* which, along with their other hit *You'll never walk alone* have become twin anthems for Liverpool.

Launched in 1951, the *Royal Iris* had been the most high profile of the Mersey Ferries 'fleet' for some 40 years. Intended as an up-market dance-cruise ship, she became known to one and all as the 'fish and chip boat'. It was as such that the Beatles performed on board her during 1961 and 1962 in five *Riverboat Shuffles* presented by the Cavern Club. Judged too expensive to repair, she was eventually pensioned off and, as at May 2016, is slowly rotting away on the River Thames in London.

The Pier Head was also the venue for a controversial Lennon concert on 5th May 1990 promoted by Yoko Ono who appeared on stage with Sean and a host of pop luminaries. Performers as diverse as Lou Reed, Cyndi Lauper, Randy Travis and Kylie Mynogue performed cover versions of Lennon hits. The event did raise more than £300,000 to enable the University of Liverpool to set up a scholarship fund to help needy students. A video of the concert *Lennon: A Tribute* was released in April 1991.

The Mersey Ferries terminal, opened in 2009, houses a **Beatles Story** satellite attraction with exhibitions to complement those at Albert Dock. The 'Beatles Story Ticket' also includes admission to this attraction. Apart from special exhibitions, there is a Fab4 store and Fab4 café.

(Turn right at the statue of King Edward VII on horseback and go between the Royal Liver and Cunard Buildings. At the traffic lights, cross the dock road into Water Street. At the top of Water Street, jutting out into the road, is Liverpool Town Hall)

The Mersey Ferries Terminal / Beatles Story. The statue on the left depicts Battle of the Atlantic, World War Two hero, Captain Johnnie Walker.

LIVERPOOL TOWN HALL: BEATLES' CIVIC RECEPTION

Water Street *(L2 3SW)*

As they stood on the balcony (pictured above left) alongside the Lord Mayor and other civic dignitaries, the Beatles received a hero's welcome from the thousands of their Merseyside fans who crowded the streets fanning out from the Town Hall.

Earlier on that Friday evening, 10 July 1964, they had headed a cavalcade cheered by nearly a quarter of a million fans as it slowly made its way from Speke Airport to the city centre and the glittering civic reception that awaited them.

From the Minstrel's Gallery, the Beatles gazed down on the specially invited guests assembled to pay homage to them in the ballroom of the City's beautiful Georgian Town Hall, built in 1754. Earlier, in the intimacy of the Lord Mayor's Parlour, they had sipped tea from bone china cups elegantly embossed with the city's Coat of Arms (pictured above right).

Later that evening, to yet more scenes of Beatlemania, they attended the northern premiere of their first film *A Hard Day's Night* at the Odeon Cinema, London Road, now demolished. They had well and truly 'arrived' in Liverpool the city of their birth.

In the ground floor Council Chamber on 7 March 1984, the City Council passed the resolution that confirmed the honour of *Freemen of the City* on the Beatles. Their names are inscribed on the list of Honorary Freemen in the Entrance Hall. Check the Liverpool Town Hall website for open days, tours and events. A visit during their 'open days' is highly recommended.

(Continue along Dale Street. Cross at North John Street. On the next block is The Temple)

CASSANOVA CLUB *The Temple, Dale Street (L2 5RL)*

Named after popular Merseybeat group, Cass and the Cassanovas, the Cassanova Club was housed for a short time in an upstairs room in the Temple building, the city's first rock venue and an unlikely one at that. Previously, in the 1950s, it was a jazz venue whose most famous guest performer, in 1955, was legendary bluesman Big Bill Broonzy. Here on a Sunday afternoon early in 1960 the Beatles played during the interval. The Cassanova Club relocated to London Road early in 1961 and the Cassanovas morphed into The Big Three.

(Turn into Temple Street to the new office building half way down the street on the left.)

THE IRON DOOR *13 Temple Street, off Dale Street (L2 5RH)*

The bronze plaque on the wall of 5 Temple Square commemorates the fact that the 19th century warehouse that once stood here was the home of the famous beat club. The Iron Door was initially opened by Geoff Hogarth as a jazz club on 9 April 1960. Eleven months later, in March 1961 when it was still known as the Liverpool Jazz Society, the Beatles played five gigs here.

In a sense, The Iron Door is Merseybeat's 'forgotten club' yet it is worth making the point that it pre-dates the Cavern as a rock and roll venue and perhaps merits its claim of being 'The Cradle of Merseybeat'. The Iron Door was the venue on 11 March 1961 for Merseyside's first 'all-nighter' staged by pioneering local rock and roll promoter Sam Leach – 12 bands played for 12 hours from 8pm on the Saturday night until 8am on Sunday morning. Mike Jackson, drummer with the Mojos, remembers stepping over a body in the cloakrooms here early one Sunday morning – it was John Lennon having a sleep. "Cold in here. isn't it?" he said, pulling the coat that served as a blanket closer to him.

The plaque names the Beatles and 14 other bands, including Kingsize Taylor and the Dominos whose leader, Teddy Taylor, performed the unveiling.

(At the bottom of Temple Street turn left into Victoria Street. Continue to the end of the street and cross the road to St John's Gardens at the rear of St George's Hall)

ST JOHN'S GARDENS *(L3 8EW)*

In the Peace Garden, near the rear of St George's Hall, a tree in memory of John Lennon, was planted in 2000 by his half-sister, Julia Baird. Four days after his death on 3 December 2001, an English oak tree in memory of George Harrison was planted on the opposite side of the Gardens between an Indian bean tree and the *Tree of Life*, appropriate given George's interests in horticulture, India and mysticism. To thwart souvenir hunters, the trees are unmarked, making it nigh impossible for visitors to locate them.

(At the top left-hand exit, enter William Brown Street. This is the cultural heart of the city centre with its World Museum Liverpool, Central Library, Walker Art Gallery and St George's Hall.)

Entrance to the Central Library. The Picton Library is the circular building to the right.

PICTON LIBRARY – PAUL'S 'FREEDOM OF THE CITY' CEREMONY

William Brown Street (L3 8EW)

Lamentably, any proposal to honour Liverpool's most famous sons created discord in the city of their birth: 'twas ever thus. Nevertheless, on 7 March 1984, Liverpool City Council managed to pass a resolution bestowing on each Beatle the Honorary Freedom of the City, the highest honour it is possible for an individual to receive from the City. Passing a resolution was one thing. Getting the Beatles to come to Liverpool to be formally made Freemen of the City was something else. Yoko finally collected John's Freedom of the City award in a tree-planting ceremony in New York's Strawberry Field in October 1998. George and Ringo's scrolls are still locked away in the City Council's safe awaiting collection!

Always the most amenable and public relations conscious of the Fab Four, Paul readily accepted the invitation. And it was in this impressive circular domed library that, on 28 November 1984, Paul McCartney MBE received the scroll that confirmed his new status as a Freeman of the City.

At that time the infamous Militant-controlled Council was steering the City towards bankruptcy. "Does this mean I get to see the books?" Paul joked as he responded to speeches by Council worthies.

Among items of Beatle interest held by the library (but rarely on display) are the baptism records of George and Ringo and a programme for the Woolton Village fete held on 6 July 1957 – when Paul and John met for the first time. The Library, which recently underwent a £50m multi award-winning redevelopment, is well worth a visit simply to stand in the entrance and look up at the atrium...stunning.

(Next door to the Picton Library is the Walker Art Gallery)

WALKER ART GALLERY *William Brown Street (L3 8EL)*

One of Stuart Sutcliffe's paintings was selected from amongst thousands of entries for the prestigious bi-annual John Moores Liverpool Exhibition held here in 1959. Moores, founder of the once-famous Littlewoods football pools, catalogue and High Street stores empire, and after whom one of the city's three universities, the Liverpool John Moores University is named, bought the painting for £65 for his

private collection. For the struggling art student it was in those days a princely sum. Stu promptly spent part of it on a down-payment for an electric bass guitar enabling him to join John, Paul and George.

Tragically, age 21, Stu died of a brain haemorrhage in the arms of his German fiance Astrid Kirchherr. He had been studying under Eduardo Paolozzi at the Hamburg College of Art. Two years later, in 1964, with Beatlemania at its height, the Walker staged an exhibition of his work. It ran from 2-24 May and was seen by over 11,000 visitors.

One of Stu's paintings, *'Hamburg Painting No.2'*, is owned by the Walker and is normally on view. Pictured (*left*) is another of Stu's *Hamburg* paintings, displayed in *The Art of the Beatles* exhibition.

In 1984 rock writer Mike Evans and I put together *The Art of the Beatles* exhibition. It ran from May to September, attracted nearly 50,000 paying visitors and was judged a great success. The fans certainly loved it. Paul contributed the drumskin for the Peter Blake *Sgt Pepper* album cover collage pictured below.

Cynthia Lennon accepted our invitation to open the exhibition and related the times when she and John, as awestruck art students, would tip toe round the Walker speaking in whispers. He would have seen the funny side of *The Art of the Beatles* show. By the Walker's standards, it was slightly irreverent – there was non-stop Beatle music and videos, a pile of bricks from the old Cavern (shades of the Tate!) and the hallowed walls displayed his once-banned 'Bag One' drawings alongside paintings from his childhood. The exhibition was later staged in Japan and Cologne.

"John and I spent many a pleasant afternoon wandering around the Walker when we were young, so going back to the 'Pool with my paintings will complete some kind of circle for me and I'm really excited about it" said Paul when the first comprehensive exhibition of his paintings in Britain, was staged here in 2002. The 60 plus paintings, sculpture and photo pieces that made up 'the art of Paul McCartney' drew comments from critics which varied from "truly surprising" to "a dog's dinner of dreadful dawbs defying description".

(At the top of William Brown Street, cross Lime Street to the Empire Theatre on the corner of London Road and Lime Street. On the next block up London Road is where the Odeon Cinema once stood.)

FORMER ODEON CINEMA *London Road (L3 5NF)*

Before it was split into a number of smaller cinemas, the Odeon was one enormous 'picture palace'. On 7 December 1963 it was the venue for two performances by the Beatles following a hectic afternoon at the nearby Empire Theatre.

On 10 July 1964, the same day that the Beatles had been honoured at a civic reception at Liverpool Town Hall, the Odeon became the setting for the northern premiere of the Beatles' first film *A Hard Day's Night*. It was a Hollywood-style event easily surpassing the film's earlier Royal premiere in London. The 1969 film, *The Magic Christian*, in which Ringo co-starred with Peter Sellers, was also given its northern premiere here.

Another glittering event took place here on the evening of 28 November 1984 when Paul and Linda McCartney attended the UK premiere of Paul's film *Give My Regards To Broad Street*. During the afternoon Paul had been made an Honorary Freeman of the City of Liverpool. The Odeon held early memories for Paul: he had saved the money to watch Bill Haley and the Comets perform live here in 1957 although a disappointed George Harrison couldn't afford the 15 shillings ticket price. The film *Backbeat*, which told the story of the Beatles' early days, was given its world premiere here on 24 March 1994.

Opened in 1934 as the Paramount cinema, the Odeon finally closed in 2008. It was demolished in 2011 and the site redeveloped as The Paramount, a 10-storey student accommodation block.

(Opposite here, above the old storefronts, was the former Cassanova Club.)

CASSANOVA CLUB / PEPPERMINT LOUNGE
London Rd/Fraser St. (L3 8HR)

The Cassanova Club transferred to Sampson and Barlow's ballroom here from its short-lived home in The Temple, Dale Street, and was opened by local promoter Sam Leach on 9 February 1961. Two days later the Beatles played the first of seven dates here.

The following week, on Valentine's night, fans paid four shillings and sixpence (about 22 pence – refreshments included) to bop to the Beatles, the Big Three, Rory Storm and the Hurricanes and Mark Peters and the Cyclones. The Cassanova Club hit the headlines 35 years later when the first-ever film footage of the Beatles came to light – half a minute of colour film without sound, reputedly shot in the club on that very night.

Later, as the Peppermint Lounge, or 'The Pep' as it was known, it continued to be a popular venue for local groups although by then the Beatles had moved on.

Further down Fraser Street was Mr Pickwick's club, the setting for the first-ever Liverpool Beatles Convention on 8/9 October 1977, masterminded by Cavern DJ Bob Wooler and the Beatles' first manager Allan Williams. My main role was to persuade the English Tourist Board to fund the event. It was my first involvement with Bob and Allan and turned out to be quite an experience!

(Return to Lime Street.)

EMPIRE THEATRE *Lime Street* (L1 1JE)

The Beatles stood in the shower of their cramped dressing room at the Empire Theatre for this photograph.

The City's biggest and most glamourous theatre where, on 9 June 1957, and again some ten days later, John Lennon's Quarrymen skiffle group competed against other local hopefuls for the chance to appear on Carroll 'Mr Star-Maker' Levis's TV show. They never made it to the finals but were more successful when, as Johnny and the Moondogs, they competed here two or three times in October 1959, performing covers of Buddy Holly hits and winning a place in the final round of auditions in Manchester in late November.

With the prospect of fame and fortune within their sights, John, Paul and George came back to Lime Street on the train from Manchester with their tails between their legs. Mr Star-Maker's auditions had run on late into the evening. They didn't have the money to stay in Manchester overnight so they had to come home before it was their turn to audition.

When they returned to play the Empire again three years later on 28th October 1962 the Beatles had really hit the big time in the eyes of their Liverpool fans, even though they took second billing to Little Richard, Craig Douglas, Kenny Lynch, Sounds Incorporated and Jet Harris.

Over the next two years the Beatles appeared here on another six occasions two of which were especially memorable. On the afternoon of 7 December 1963, they gave a special concert for 2,500 members of their Northern Area Fan Club and took part in the filming of Juke Box Jury to the added delight of those same fans. That evening, as the Beatles gave two concerts at the Odeon cinema round the corner from the Empire, 23 million television viewers saw the unique 'Juke Box Jury' panel of John, Paul, George and Ringo pass judgement on a batch of the latest record releases.

The Beatles' 11th and final appearance at the Empire took place on 5th December 1965. Little did their adoring army of local fans realise that it was also to be the very last time their idols were to perform in Liverpool as a group. However, George was back on stage here in 1969 with Delaney & Bonnie, Paul played here in 1973 and again in 1975 with his band Wings. And Ringo with his All Starr Band, featuring son Zak also on drums, was here in 1992 and again in 2011.

Paul came on stage here at the end of the 'A Concert For George' tribute on 24 February 2002, reminisced about his old friend and sang 'Yesterday'.

19

Directly opposite the Empire is St George's Hall, shown above, with the Steble Fountain right.

ST. GEORGE'S HALL *Lime Street (L1 1JJ)*

Opened in 1854, St George's Hall is ranked as one of the finest Graeco-Roman style buildings in the world and is a fitting memorial to its 23 year-old architect, Harvey Lonsdale Elmes. A visit is highly recommended.

On 13 May 1960 this was the setting for a wild Liverpool Arts Ball, organised by Allan Williams and based on the famous Chelsea Arts Ball. He commissioned the Beatles to design and make decorative floats – one was in the shape of a guitar – which were destined to be destroyed by the revellers during the course of the evening. The ball ended in chaos with the hall's outraged owners, Liverpool City Council, swearing "never again". But memories are short and they allowed the 1984 Beatles Convention to take place here, this time without incident.

On the Sunday following John's murder on 8 December 1980, tens of thousands of grieving fans held an emotional vigil on the plateau in front of the hall where, two decades earlier, along with Paul and George and fellow art student Stu Sutcliffe, he had struggled with their carnival floats. The crowds were back on the plateau again for a candlelit vigil on 3 December 2001 to mark the untimely death of George Harrison three days earlier.

On 11 January 2008, Ringo was the star turn at the launch of Liverpool's reign as 'European Capital of Culture 2008'. Thousands watched as he performed the title song of his new album *Liverpool 8* from the roof of St George's Hall. *(Continue along Lime Street)*

LIME STREET TRAIN STATION *(L1 1JD)*

"Oh Maggie May, they have taken her away and she'll never walk down Lime Street any more." sang John in the Beatles' version of the famous Liverpool folk song *Maggie May*. This was a place of many Beatle comings and goings in the early 60s; more particularly, Brian Epstein made frequent trips to London in a vain attempt to interest record companies in the Beatles...until, in June 1962, they auditioned for EMI in the form of George Martin and, as they say, the rest is history.

Beatles-era photograph of Lime Street Station with the 'Punch and Judy' on the right. Paul: "John and I used to wait at Lime Street Station in a little coffee bar called Punch and Judy. We used to wait for Brian arriving back from London, and when he'd come off the train we'd take a look at his face to see if it was good news or bad, and it was bad. It was always bad. He'd be, like, 'Sorry'. We'd go, 'Oh,' and we'd have a cup of coffee and discuss what had happened."

(Look across the road to the left where you will see the Royal Court Theatre, Roe Street. The Beatles never performed there but in November 1979 Wings played four nights on the run, the first gig being an exclusive free concert given by Paul for masters and pupils from his old school, the Liverpool Institute. Julian Lennon also performed here in 1989. Continue along Lime Street to its junction with Elliot Street. Look to the left and you will see Weatherspoons, formerly Blacklers store.)

FORMER BLACKLERS STORE *Great Charlotte Street/Elliot Street. Now the Richard John Blackler, a Weatherspoon pub (L1 1HU)*

After leaving school George Harrison served a brief apprenticeship here as an electrician from November 1959 to May 1960 when he packed it in to join the Silver Beetles on their tour of Scotland with Johnny Gentle – "I got a job cleaning all the lights with a paint brush, all those tubes to keep clean, and at Christmas I kept the Grotto clean." But, on at least one occasion, George was to be found serving behind the counter in Blacklers' modest record 'department'.

His time at Blacklers also taught him two other dubious but useful 'skills' – how to skive off the job and how to down fourteen pints of beer, three rum and blackcurrants and two burgers from the local Wimpey's, all in one session. Surely an exaggeration?!

NEMS opened their first city centre branch at 50 Great Charlotte Street, next door to a raucous Yates's Wine Lodge, in late 1957. Brian Epstein ran the record section with military precision and made such a success of it that his father was encouraged to open another, bigger, store in Whitechapel in May 1960.

(Continue along Lime Street.)

Above left: the Adelphi Hotel and, far left, the Vines public house, known as 'The Big House'.
Above right: afternoon tea can be taken in the Edwardian splendour of the main lounge.

BRITANNIA ADELPHI HOTEL *Ranelagh Place (L3 5UL)*

Built in 1914 at a time when Liverpool was the country's premier port for transatlantic passengers, the Adelphi is the last remaining grand old Liverpool hotel.

It is the setting for the annual Beatles Convention held at the end of August every year and attended by fans from all over the world. The American conventions are bigger and slicker affairs but the Liverpool event has that extra special ingredient that can't be found anywhere else in the world – after all, it is held 'In the town where they were born'.

The Beatles never stayed here but Yoko and Sean stopped off in 1990 when they were in Liverpool for John's memorial concert at the Pier Head. The hotel achieved nationwide notoriety in 1997 as the subject of the warts-and-all documentary series *Hotel* which portrayed it in a very poor light. Sadly, the poor old Adelphi, which would have enormous potential under a different operator, continues to attract unfavourable revues on travel websites such as TripAdvisor where over 40% of guests rate it as either 'poor' or 'terrible'. The Mayor of Liverpool even threatened to slap a Compulsory Purchase Order on it if they didn't pull their socks up.

(Look across the street to the former Lewis's store building opposite)

FORMER LEWIS'S STORE *Ranalegh Street (L1 1JX)*

The top floor of this former iconic department store, the biggest in Liverpool in its day, was the setting for a Beatles performance at a staff 'Young Idea Dance' for the '527 Club' on 28 November 1962. And, for a few weeks, Paul even worked as a 'second man' on a delivery van for Lewis's.

John and Cynthia regularly met under the store's dramatic statue of a naked man arms reaching heavenward. This once-controversial figure (known to many Liverpudlians, for obvious reasons, as 'Dickie Lewis') represents 'Liverpool Resurgent' and was sculpted by Epstein – Jacob, not Brian! After 154 years, Lewis's finally closed in 2010; the building is being incorporated into a much larger 'Central Village' mixed use redevelopment scheme.

(Cross at the traffic lights and continue up the right hand side of Mount Pleasant)

FORMER REGISTRY OFFICE: JOHN AND CYNTHIA'S WEDDING

64 Mount Pleasant *(L3 5TB)*

On Thursday 23 August 1962 a strange little ceremony was performed here, a former Georgian town house built in 1773. The participants were John, Paul, George, Brian Epstein and Cynthia and her brother and his wife. The occasion? The marriage of Beatle John, aged 21 to his 22 year-old pregnant art school girlfriend Cynthia Powell. The brief ceremony was conducted to the ear-splitting accompaniment of a pneumatic drill operated by a workman in the building next door. Ringo wasn't there. He'd only just joined the Beatles and hadn't been invited; John didn't even tell him he'd got married that day.

After the brief ceremony, they had all sprinted down the hill in the pouring rain to queue in Reece's restaurant for the wedding breakfast. John spent his wedding night playing a gig with the Beatles in Chester. There was to be no proper honeymoon either. The Beatles' crowded diary of engagements wouldn't allow it. It was a marriage destined not to last very long. Six years later, on 8 November 1968, it ended in the divorce court following John's admitted adultery with his 'soul-mate', the Japanese artist Yoko Ono.

In this same Registry Office 24 years earlier, on 3 December 1938, John's mother Julia, a cinema usherette, had married ship's steward Freddie Lennon. The next day Freddie sailed off to the West Indies. Julia saw little of him during their brief and stormy marriage and, by the time John was 18 months old, father Freddie had left them both for good. Also, Ringo's mother, Elsie, married her second husband Harry Graves here on 17 April 1954.

(Continue to the traffic lights at the junction of Mount Pleasant and Rodney Street. Just around the corner, on the right is No. 4)

4 RODNEY STREET – BRIAN EPSTEIN'S BIRTHPLACE *(L1 2TZ)*

Elegantly Georgian, Rodney Street is Liverpool's equivalent of London's 'street of doctors', Harley Street. No. 4 was the home of James Maury. He was appointed as America's very first Consul in Europe by George Washington in 1790 and was U.S. Consul in Liverpool from that year until 1829. Of more interest to Beatle fans, it was once a private nursing home and the birthplace, on 19 September 1934, of Brian Samuel Epstein –

pronounced 'Epsteen' but known to the Beatles and his other Merseybeat groups simply as 'Eppy'. To the staff of his NEMS records shops he was the more formal 'Mr Brian'.

His parents, Harry and Queenie, were prosperous middle-class Jews and could afford a live-in nanny for Brian at their very 'des res' (desirable residence) at the posh end of Queens Drive (see p68).

At the height of the Beatles' success a radio interviewer asked Brian – "Were you born in Liverpool?" He replied, "I would have said it was essential.", the clear inference being that he could not have steered the Beatles to fame and fortune had he not been a fellow Liverpudlian.

If anyone could lay claim to the accolade 'The Fifth Beatle', it was this man. Indeed, during an interview, Paul McCartney explained – "If anyone was the fifth Beatle it was Brian. People talked about George Martin as being the fifth Beatle because of his musical involvement but, particularly in the early days, Brian was very much part of the group."

(Continue to the top of Mount Pleasant. The R. C. Cathedral is on the opposite side of the road; no Beatle connections but it is a modern classic and should definitely be visited.)

ROMAN CATHOLIC CATHEDRAL **Mount Pleasant (L3 5TQ)**

Visitors to the R.C. Cathedral, or the Metropolitan Cathedral of Christ the King to give it its full title, either like it or they don't. From the outside it's a controversial building, architecturally, but reserve your judgement until you've looked inside. Most critics are stunned into silence.

Completed in 1967, it is known to irreverent Liverpudlians as 'Paddy's Wigwam' ('Paddy'? – The city has a large Irish Catholic population). It has also been nick-named 'The Mersey Funnel' and 'The Pope's Launching Pad'.

Originally the intention in the 1930s was to build a cathedral second only in size to St Peter's, Rome, with room for 10,000 worshippers. However, the cost spiralled to over £1billion by today's values and it was abandoned with only the Lutyens crypt, designed by Sir Edwin Lutyens, completed. This can be visited Monday to Saturday.

You'll also find a café, gift shop and toilets here.

THIS IS NOT HERE

To Julia Lennon, nee Stanley, a son

John Lennon

(1940-80)
born here in the former
Liverpool Maternity Hospital
6.30pm 9 October 1940

PLAQUE PLACED BY
NORTHERN DESIGN UNIT
9 OCTOBER 2000

(Cross the traffic lights at the junction of Mount Pleasant and Hope Street into Oxford Street. The next street along is Arrad Street. Keep to the left of 'the Font' bar and you will see the former Maternity Hospital, known to many older Liverpudlians as 'The Stork Hotel'. Closed in 1995, it has since been converted into apartments.)

FORMER OXFORD STREET MATERNITY HOSPITAL — JOHN LENNON'S BIRTHPLACE *now part of Unite Student Village (L7 7AG)*

Here, in the old main building, at around 6.30pm on Wednesday, 9 October 1940, arguably Liverpool's most famous son, John Winston Lennon, was born. No memorial plaque was erected over his bed; nobody can even remember which ward he was born in! His Aunt Mimi favoured the name John and Winston was no doubt chosen as a patriotic tribute to Britain's great wartime leader Winston Churchill who was that very day elected leader of the Conservative Party.

On Saturday 12 October this notice of John's birth appeared in the Liverpool Echo:

> LENNON-October 9, in hospital to JULIA (nee Stanley), wife of
> ALFRED LENNON, Merchant Navy (at sea), a son-9 Newcastle
> Road.

John's own zany account of his birth, written for the *Mersey Beat* newspaper, is more interesting – "I was bored on the 9 October 1940, when, I believe, the Nasties were still booming us, led by Madalf Heatlump (who only had one). Anyway they didn't get me..."

Most accounts of John's birth tell of Aunt Mimi dodging shrapnel as she ran through the bomb-torn streets of Liverpool to see the new baby, who had to be placed under the bed during the air raid. It's a nice, whimsical, oft-told tale... but a tall one for all that. Official war records confirm that the Luftwaffe gave Liverpool a miss that particular night.

(Retrace your steps and turn left into Hope Street. It is neat that Liverpool can boast two world-class cathedrals, each at either end of a street called 'Hope'.)

EVERYMAN THEATRE
Hope Street (L1 9BH)

What you see today is the third Everyman Theatre to have stood on this site; this completely rebuilt Everyman opened in 2013 at a cost of £28m. The original building, dating from 1837 had been a dissenters' chapel, church, public concert hall and a cinema before ending its days as the first Everyman Theatre in 1975. Although Merseybeat groups started to appear from late 1962, the Beatles never played here. However, it is known that George and Ringo came along to at least one of the poetry readings that were a feature of Liverpool's famous poetry scene in the

Liverpool actor Mark McGann played John in the hit production of the play 'Lennon'.

60s . "Liverpool is the centre of all human consciousness" – declared Allen Ginsberg, American poet and leading apostle of the beat generation. Liverpudlians loved him for it even though they didn't have a clue what he was talking about. Nor did they understand Carl Gustav Jung, the celebrated Swiss philosopher, when he pronounced, following a dream that changed his life, that "Liverpool is the Pool of Life."

More significantly, Paul turned 'performance poet' on 21 March 2001 when he gave a reading of some of the poems from his first anthology *Blackbird Singing* to an audience of 400 here at the second Everyman Theatre. Earlier that day, some 3,000 fans had queued at WH Smith's bookshop in Church Street for a chance to meet Paul and buy a signed copy of *Blackbird Singing*.

The Everyman's real Beatle pedigree is to be found in the plays premiered here. *John, Paul, George, Ringo and Bert* by Liverpool playwright Willy Russell, of *Shirley Valentine*, *Educating Rita* and *Blood Brothers* fame, had its world premiere here in 1974. It played to capacity houses for six weeks before transferring to the West End of London and then, in 1982, off-Broadway, New York, where it received indifferent reviews.

This was followed in 1981, just six months after John was shot dead, by the premiere of *Lennon*, a musical play devised and directed by Bob Eaton. In collaboration with Yoko Ono, he reprised the play at Liverpool's Royal Court Theatre 70 years after John's birth and 30 years after his death.

(Continue along Hope Street to its junction with Hardman Street. On the opposite side of the road is one of John Lennon's favourite pubs, the 'Phil'.)

PHILHARMONIC PUB
Hope Street (L1 9BX)

Liverpool's most famous Victorian pub was frequented by the Beatles as an alternative to their regular pub 'Ye Cracke' a short distance further along Hope Street. John later bemoaned the fact that the price of fame was…"not being able to go to the *Phil* for a drink". Paul played an impromptu gig in the pub's Dining Room here on 19 June

2018 as part of the Late Late Show's Carpool Karaoke show with James Corden, to the surprise and delight of unsuspecting fans.

(Cross at the traffic lights to the Philharmonic Hall. If you look up Hardman Street you will see, on the opposite side of the road, the Liverpool Community College Arts Centre, built on the site of the Royal Liverpool Children's Hospital.)

ROYAL LIVERPOOL CHILDREN'S HOSPITAL

Myrtle Street *(L7 7JA)*
Demolished and replaced by Liverpool Community College's Arts Centre

When he was nearly seven years old Ringo was rushed here with violent stomach pains. His appendix had burst. Peritonitis set in and he slipped into a dangerous coma that was to last ten weeks; three times doctors told his mother that he would not make it through the night. He remained here for the best part of a year. Dogged by bad luck, he even managed to fall out of bed and open up the scars from his operation, just when he was about to return to his home in the nearby Dingle.

Illness struck Ringo down yet again when he was nearly fourteen, this time with pleurisy. During his ten-week stay there his pleurisy developed into tuberculosis (TB). He was despatched to the hospital's sanatorium (now demolished) at Heswall with its open air wards looking out over the Dee estuary and the Welsh Hills beyond. There he caught yet another bug...drumming.

His childhood friend and close neighbour Marie Maguire (now Marie Crawford and an official BeatleGuide) was a regular visitor to Heswall during his near two-year hospitalisation and remembers him as an enthusiastic member of the ward band. On one occasion she presented a delighted Ringo with drummer Eric Delaney's hit record *Oranges and Lemons*. It was Marie who had taught the sickly Ringo, or 'Richy' as he was known to everyone in those days, to read and write. Illness had robbed him of even a basic education.

PHILHARMONIC HALL **Hope Street** *(L1 9BP)*

In common with most Liverpool school children, each member of the Beatles no doubt attended at least one concert at the 'Phil' by the RLPO (Royal Liverpool Philharmonic Orchestra) during the 50s.

From the late 50s it became a popular venue for pop groups, but not the Beatles. One of their biggest early influences, Buddy Holly and the Crickets, played here on 25 March 1958, but for some inexplicable reason none of the Beatles went to their hero's concert that night. The publishing rights to Holly's song catalogue are now owned by one of his biggest fans, Paul McCartney.

The by-now famous George was here in 1963 as a panelist judging the final of the Lancashire and Cheshire Beat Group Competition. Also on the jury was Dick Rowe,

forever remembered as 'the man who turned down the Beatles'. George had been impressed by a new R & B group he'd seen in London and suggested that Rowe should sign them up. The band?...the Rolling Stones. This time Rowe does the right thing and takes George's advice.

From time to time the hall echoes to orchestral versions of Beatles' classics, most notably when their recording manager George Martin conducted the orchestra.

To celebrate the orchestra's 150th anniversary in 1991, Paul McCartney wrote a full-length orchestral symphony *Liverpool Oratorio* in collaboration with American-born composer Carl Davis. Although rehearsals took place here, the premiere was staged in the Anglican Cathedral on 28 and 29 June. Fittingly, after being performed in twenty countries, the 100th performance took place here in September 1996 with the proud McCartney in attendance.

A pun on his 'working class' Liverpool roots, *Working Classical*, Paul's third orchestral work (the second was *Standing Stone*), performed by the London Symphony Orchestra with the Loma Mar Quartet, was premiered here on 16 October 1999. Paul and members of his family were in the audience. At around the same time, and in stark contrast to his late interest in orchestral and chamber music, Paul released *Run Devil Run*, comprised almost entirely of cover versions of rock and roll classics that influenced him as a teenager growing up in Liverpool in the 1950s .

The 1968 film *Yellow Submarine*, digitally enhanced and with a re-mixed soundtrack, was given its UK premier here on 14 September 1999 and, on 2 July 2001, Yoko Ono walked on stage to be made a Doctor of Laws by the University of Liverpool in recognition of her work as a conceptual artist and for the John Lennon Memorial Scholarship which she helped establish in 1991 to assist the higher education of needy students. Receiving her honorary degree she remarked - "You have no idea what this means to me, for this is not any city, this is Liverpool. It is my husband John's birthplace and the place that he never stopped talking about all his life."

(Continue along Hope Street and turn left into Falkner Street. No 36 is on the right hand side, near the far end of the street.)

36 FALKNER STREET — JOHN & CYNTHIA'S HONEYMOON FLAT
(L8 7PZ)

The Beatles' manager Brian Epstein rented, but hardly ever used, the ground floor flat of this house. When John and Cynthia got married in August 1962, Brian let them honeymoon at the flat until they found a place of their own. Eventually, John and Cyn moved back to *Mendips* his Aunt Mimi's house in Menlove Avenue.

Whilst living here John had written *Do you want to know a secret?*, sung by George on the *Please, Please Me* album. It was also the song which had propelled another of Epstein's Merseybeat groups, Billy J Kramer and the Dakotas, to the top of the charts. John recalled the time he wrote the song:

"I was in the first apartment I'd ever had that wasn't shared by fourteen other students – gals and guys at art school. I'd just married Cyn and Brian Epstein gave us his secret little apartment that he kept in Liverpool for his sexual liaisons separate from his home life. And he let Cyn and I have that apartment."

Significantly, it was in this very flat in September that year that Brian sat John and Paul down to explain their draft 11-clause music publishing contract which would give Lennon and McCartney equal credit for sheet music, records, publicity etc. Although they agreed a proviso that the name of the principal author would go first when crediting any song, in practice this never happened and it was 'Lennon/McCartney' from that time on.

(Re-trace your steps to Hope Street and cross over into Rice Street)

'YE CRACKE'

Rice Street *(L1 9BB)*

The local pub for students from the nearby Art College and, occasionally, mature looking schoolboys from the Liverpool Institute. 'Black Velvets' would be drunk by John, Stuart Sutcliffe and their other student cronies in boisterous lunchtime drinking bouts. John's romance with fellow art student Cynthia Powell from posh 'over the water' Hoylake on the Wirral also blossomed here.

Frequently, they would be joined by their lecturer and ally, Arthur Ballard, who even conducted tutorials in the back room of the pub. John, who had recently lost his mother in an horrific road accident, drowned his sorrows here and often returned to the Art College in a drunken state. He later admitted: "When I went to art college in Liverpool, you know, it was mainly one long drinking session."

Drinking on one occasion was temporarily abandoned when the then-famous Liverpool-born film star John Gregson appeared outside the pub. Lennon, in typically unconventional fashion, managed to get his autograph...on a dirty old boot that was lying around. On another occasion John pretended to 'swim' in pools of beer on the bar room floor.

A commemorative plaque inside the pub marks the occasion when, in June 1960, four art students (John Lennon, Stuart Sutcliffe, Bill Harry and Rod Murray) attended a poetry reading by Royston Ellis. The four came here to discuss what they had heard. They were unimpressed and decided to put Liverpool on the map, each in his own way as 'The Dissenters'.

(Return to Hope Street and its junction with Mount Street)

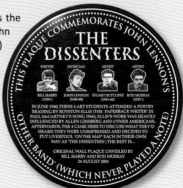

FORMER LIVERPOOL INSTITUTE — PAUL & GEORGE'S HIGH SCHOOL, NOW LIVERPOOL INSTITUTE FOR PERFORMING ART (LIPA) *Mount Street (L1 9HF)*

Since 1837 this building had been home to the Liverpool Institute, or the 'Innie' as it was known, and was the city's most prestigious high school for boys. It was every Liverpool mother's dream that her son would pass the eleven-plus examination and win one of the prized places here even though he would be branded a 'college pudding' by his lesser talented and no doubt envious mates.

The Innie's two most famous sons were Paul and George. Academically, they were poles apart. Paul had already been here a year when George started in 1954; the Innie was to be their school until they left for Hamburg in 1960. Disinterested and rebellious from the start, George frittered away his opportunities and failed all his exams. He made a mockery of his school uniform by wearing tight drainpipe trousers and, once, a canary yellow waistcoat under his black school blazer. Not for George the regulation 'short back and sides' haircut. He grew his hair as long as he could, piled high in the Elvis and Tony Curtis styles of the day and topped by the universally hated, but compulsory, school cap.

"A boy with little academic ability. Art is the only subject at which he has made any effort." said a school report card, prepared in April 1959 for the Liverpool Youth Employment Bureau. It also noted that he was in the bottom five in his form and that he had expressed a desire to be a 'student fitter'.

Whilst by no means an enthusiastic scholar, Paul was a natural student with the knack of being able to listen to the radio and do his school homework at the same time. He did just enough to get a respectable five GCE 'O' level and one 'A' level passes, failing in History, Geography, Scripture and German. One of his old maths

April 1956, the Liverpool Institute's Lower School (part 1)

Mike McCartney, Paul's younger brother   *Paul McCartney*

books from Class 4B, filled with doodles and scribbles, fetched £23,000 at a Tokyo auction in 1997.

The Institute had one big plus for Paul and George. It was next door to the Art College, venue for practice sessions with John Lennon and Stu Sutcliffe.

Following its closure in 1985, the Institute was given a new lease of life when Paul announced plans to convert it into a 'School of Fame' or, to give it its full and proper title, 'The Liverpool Institute for Performing Arts' – 'LIPA' for short. "The initial reason for my involvement with LIPA was the building. It was my old school. When I saw for myself the state it had reached as an abandoned building, I wanted to save it."

From drawing board to official opening took six years, the process being kicked off by a £1 million pound personal donation from Paul. This was followed by the pennies of Liverpool schoolchildren and the millions of pounds of sponsorship ploughed in by Grundig. Even the Queen and celebrities such as Eddie Murphy, Jane Fonda, Ralph Lauren and David Hockney contributed towards the £12 million cost of the venture.

The first two hundred students, chosen from applications that flooded in from around the world, started their three-year degree courses in January 1996. Towards the end of that first month, Paul McCartney, watched by Beatles record producer, George Martin and Chief Executive, Mark Featherstone Witty, officially inaugurated LIPA by cutting a giant cake in the shape of his old school. On the same occasion, Paul's old school assembly hall (now a 450-seat working theatre) was named the Paul McCartney Auditorium. But the real icing on the cake came when the Queen officially opened LIPA in May 1996. And when Paul was knighted the following year, he made his acceptance speech here.

Paul continues his active involvement with LIPA to this day, attending its graduation ceremonies and giving master classes to its students.

The late Neil Aspinall, the Beatles' Road Manager

Len Garry bass player with the Quarrymen

Don Andrew and the late Colin Manley, bass player and lead guitarist, respectively, of the Remo Four

FORMER LIVERPOOL COLLEGE OF ART — JOHN AND CYNTHIA'S ART COLLEGE *Hope Street (L1 9DZ)*

Clutching a portfolio of his work from Quarry Bank High School and wearing his dead Uncle George's sports jacket and a collar and tie specially for the occasion, John scraped through the interview and was accepted as a student here in Summer, 1957.

The college was a big disappointment to the idealistic 17-year old Lennon. He was immediately strapped into the straightjacket of the lettering class with its overriding requirement for neatness and precision. John loathed it. It was totally alien to his restless, free-roaming spirit.

The only tutor to be on the same wavelength as John was Arthur Ballard who observed: "He draws naturally. As a conventional art student he was not very good but as an artist, which is very much more important, he was very talented."

John himself later said of the three years he spent here: "All I ever learned in art school was about Van Gogh and stuff. They didn't teach me anything about Marcel Duchamp which I despised them for."

It was here that he struck up a close friendship with the very talented Stuart Sutcliffe and met his future wife Cynthia Powell. Polite and twin set prim, she must have appeared an unlikely partner for the disruptive and aggressive 'teddy boy' Lennon with his drainpipe trousers, long drape jacket, sideburns and D.A. (duck's arse) hairstyle.

At an end of term college party, Lennon sounded her out for a date. Awkwardly, Cynthia explained: "I'm awfully sorry, but I'm engaged to this fellow in Hoylake." to which Lennon acidly retorted: "I didn't ask you to marry me did I?" However, she did accept an invitation to join him and his mates for a drink in 'Ye Cracke' pub. After

Liverpool City Centre

April 1956, the Liverpool Institute's Lower School (part 2)

The late Ivan Vaughan, John's boyhood friend and, briefly, base player with the Quarrymen.

(Top) Peter Sissons, BBC Television newsreader. (Below) the late Alan 'Dusty' Durband, Paul's English master and one Chairman of the Everyman Theatre.

Left: Cynthia Lennon at the opening of the Art of the Beatles exhibition in 1984. Right: John posed for fellow student, Ann Mason, in this unique and unusual portrait. Unusual? Short-sighted and vain, John hated to be seen wearing his spectacles. Cynthia died on 1 April 2015.

the drinking session they went back to Stu Sutcliffe's flat and made love. From then on their infatuation was mutual. They became inseparable. Their relationship was to end in acrimony in 1968 following John's affair with the Japanese artist Yoko Ono. He had first met Yoko in November 1966 at a private preview of her avant-garde art exhibition at London's Indica Gallery.

Sometimes an angel, more often a devil, his years at art college were difficult ones. As John later admitted: "I was in a sort of blind rage for two years. I was either drunk or fighting...There was something the matter with me."

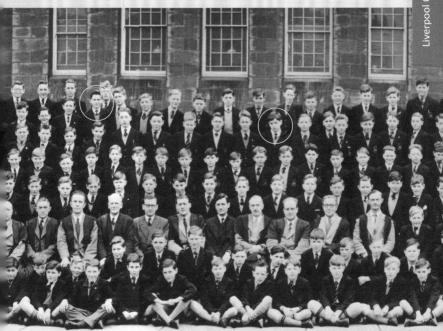

George Harrison

Les Chadwick, bass guitarist with Gerry and the Pacemakers.

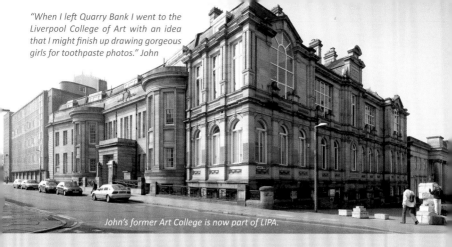

"When I left Quarry Bank I went to the Liverpool College of Art with an idea that I might finish up drawing gorgeous girls for toothpaste photos." John

John's former Art College is now part of LIPA.

The archetypal 'angry young man' both amused and appalled his fellow students with his grim humour, mostly aimed at disabled or old people. "Some people will do anything to get out of the army." he'd shout after cripples. Cruel drawings showed women cooing "Aren't they lovely." over babies with horribly contorted faces. On the day the Pope died a Lennon cartoon showed him locked outside the gates of Heaven with the caption – "But I'm the Pope I tell you!"

In the basement was the college canteen, arched and dimly lit and reminiscent of the Cavern. Here, on the stage at the back, John, Cyn and Stu, joined by Paul and George with fish and chips from the local 'chippy', would gather for practice sessions.

Some of the embryonic Beatles' earliest gigs were played here in the hall during Saturday night college dances. When they set off for Hamburg, they 'borrowed' the college's amplifier.

On a snowy 24 January 1984, Yoko brought Sean on a 'pilgrimage' to Liverpool to see some of his father's old haunts. They called here and generously presented the college with a complete set of John's *Bag One* lithographs. Rather embarrassingly, the valuable gift was later stolen from the college library. Their trip echoed an earlier pilgrimage Yoko and John had made to Liverpool in 1970. It was to be his last visit to the city.

To expand its teaching facilities, LIPA bought the old Liverpool College of Art in March 2012 for £3.7m thus uniting two historic buildings where four Beatles were educated (John, Paul, George and original bass player Stu Sutcliffe).

(At the next junction, turn left into Canning Street then right into Percy Street.)

9 PERCY STREET – STU SUTCLIFFE'S FLAT *(L8 7LT)*

Here in the rear of the first floor of No 9 was the one-room flat occupied by John's art college friends, Stu Sutcliffe, the Beatles' first bass player, often referred to as 'The Fifth Beatle', and fellow art college student Rod Murray. With his James Dean-like persona, Stu epitomised the romantic image of 'the sensitive artist'. He was regarded as 'brilliant' by his tutor Arthur Ballard, who gave him personal tuition here. Stu and Rod were eventually evicted by their furious landlady for painting and burning her furniture and fittings. They moved their sparse possessions around the corner to Gambier Terrace.

(Return to the junction of Canning Street and Hope Street. Here there is a gated entrance to Gambier Terrace.)

Percy Street: Georgian elegance.

3 GAMBIER TERRACE *(L1 7BG)*

Much against his Aunt Mimi's advice, John left the comforts of Mendips to share a flat here in 1960 with Stu Sutcliffe, Rod Murray and other students from art college. It was also a good place to spend time with Cynthia. Many was the night she spent here with John having hoodwinked her mother into believing she was staying over with a girlfriend.

The flat was an ideal place for John and Stu to draw and paint together and for the Beatles to rehearse; soon they would be off to Hamburg.

When John and Stu set off for Hamburg from here with the rest of the Beatles in August 1960, John left all his possessions with Rod. A year later he suggested to Rod that he should keep anything he wanted and throw the rest away. He kept only two items and in 1984 at Sotheby's Rock and Roll Memorabilia auction in London he sold one of John's school exercise books containing 16 pages of poetry, prose, drawings and cartoons for £16,000. The value, in artistic terms alone, of the material thrown away by Rod does not bear thinking about.

It was here in Gambier Terrace that, influenced by the name of Buddy Holly's Crickets, John bounced around possible names with Stu before finally settling on the name that the band would be called in future – The Beatles.

(The apartments in Gambier Terrace have splendid views of what is, by reason of its sheer size and hilltop position, Liverpool's most prominent building, the Anglican Cathedral. The entrance can be found down the hill near the junction of Upper Duke Street and Rodney Street.)

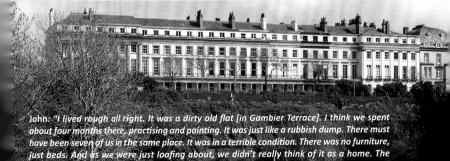
John: *"I lived rough all right. It was a dirty old flat [in Gambier Terrace]. I think we spent about four months there, practising and painting. It was just like a rubbish dump. There must have been seven of us in the same place. It was in a terrible condition. There was no furniture, just beds. And as we were just loafing about, we didn't really think of it as a home. The others tried to tidy it up a bit but we didn't bother – except I think I bought a piece of carpet or something. I left all my gear there when I went to Hamburg."*

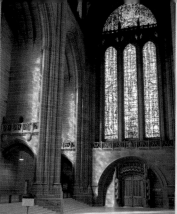

LIVERPOOL CATHEDRAL
Upper Duke Street (L1 7AZ)

This monumental building is the city's Anglican Cathedral. It was here that a Beatle with the face of an angel, was rejected because his singing voice was not thought good enough. In 1953 Paul McCartney auditioned here for a place in the cathedral choir but his rendition of the classic Christmas carol *Once in Royal David's City* failed to impress the choirmaster. In a delicious touch of irony he returned in June 1991 for the world premiere of the partly auto-biographical *Liverpool Oratorio,* the symphony he wrote in collaboration with Carl Davis to celebrate the 150th anniversary of the Royal Liverpool Philharmonic Orchestra. He was back here again in April 2008 for the northern premiere of his choral work *Ecce Cor Meum* (Behold My Heart), dedicated to first wife Linda.

Paul recalled that, as a schoolboy at the Liverpool Institute opposite, he (and John) would play truant to sunbathe and smoke ciggies on gravestones in the wonderfully atmospheric old St James Cemetery, gentrified in the 1970s to emerge as the Cathedral Gardens you see today.

It's a jaw-dropper of a building, the biggest cathedral in Britain and, after St John the Divine in New York, the largest Anglican cathedral in the world – Nelson's Column in Trafalgar Square would easily fit inside its tower and its largest bell is bigger than Big Ben. On Sunday 29 March 1981 it became the fitting venue for a special memorial service when the people of Liverpool paid their official last respects to John Lennon. During this moving 'Festival of Peace' a selection of Lennon and McCartney songs was played on the cathedral's mighty 10,268-pipe organ, the largest in Britain.

There are spectacular views over the city from atop the 331ft tower and there is a good giftshop and café. Needless to say, a visit is a 'must'.

(Continue down the hill to the traffic lights. Note the spectacular Chinese arch, the biggest in the world outside mainland China, and a symbol of Liverpool's Chinatown, the oldest in Europe. Straight ahead is Duke Street. Number 139 was once 'Joe's Cafe', a late night eating and meeting place during the Merseybeat era for the Beatles and other musicians. The owner, Joe Davey, subsequently became the owner of the Cavern during its declining years. Near the bottom of the street, at number 28, was the Cabaret Club which passed for sophistication in the Liverpool of the early 60s. Although they socialised here, the Beatles only played the venue once, on 25 July 1962, to an unappreciative audience. Cross to the right into Berry Street and continue along to Seel Street, on the opposite side of the road. Near the top of Seel Street, on the left hand side, is the Blue Angel club.)

Allan Williams presents a fan with a copy of his book 'The Fool On The Hill'. Allan died on 30 December 2016, aged 86.

BLUE ANGEL CLUB

108 Seel Street *(L1 4BL)*

Previously called the Wyvern Social Club, this was the setting for two legendary auditions. In 1960, London rock impresario Larry Parnes was looking for a band to back his star protégé Billy Fury. The Silver Beetles, with 'borrowed' drummer Johnny Hutchinson of Cass and the Cassanovas (later the Big Three), didn't pass the audition held on 10th May in the dingy basement. But they obviously impressed Parnes, despite Stu's less than adequate bass playing. He later hired them for a tour of Scotland with one of his other stars, fellow Liverpudlian Johnny Gentle.

Billy Fury was Liverpool's first rock and roll star and had been appearing in the UK charts since the beginning of 1959. Small wonder that a star-struck John Lennon had asked Billy for his autograph. Also watching the five groups being auditioned that day was Rory Storm, leader of Rory Storm and the Hurricanes...whose drummer was Ringo Starr.

Pete Best was drummer with his Casbah-based group the Blackjacks when Paul telephoned that Summer to invite him to join the Beatles for their first trip to Hamburg. But first he had to audition here on 12th August 1960 prior to joining John, Paul, George and Stu. Four days later they all set off for Hamburg.

The following year, now as the Blue Angel, the club was being run by the Beatles' 'manager' Allan Williams. The 'Blue' became *the* place for Liverpool musicians including the Beatles, although for a time Williams banned them from the club for non-payment of his manager's commission. It was also the natural choice for other stars visiting Liverpool. In those days you could have rubbed shoulders with the likes of the Rolling Stones, Bob Dylan, Judy Garland and Cilla Black.

(Continue along Berry Street to the next set of traffic lights at the junction of Bold Street and Renshaw Street.)

81A RENSHAW STREET — FORMER OFFICE OF 'MERSEY BEAT' NEWSPAPER *(L1 2SJ)*

The *Mersey Beat* newspaper was an avidly read guide to the local music scene produced from 1961 to 1964 by Bill Harry, an art college friend of John and Stu, in an office above David Land's wine merchant's shop (now the Renshaw Café), next door but one to the Roscoe Arms pub.

Liverpool City Centre

Left: former office of Mersey Beat newspaper; Right: Bill Harry photographed in 2005 in the reconstruction of the Mersey Beat office in the Beatles Story, Albert Dock.

The second page of the first edition, published on 6 July 1961, featured a typically Lennonesque article under the headline – 'Being a Short Diversion on the Dubious Origins of Beatles'. He explained how the Beatles came by their name...It came in a vision – a man appeared on a flaming pie and said unto them "From this day on you are Beatles with an A." *Flaming Pie* was also the title Paul gave to his 1997 album.

Until its demise some 90 editions later Bill's beat scene 'bible' recorded the Beatles' rise to fame. Frequent callers and regular contributors to the *Mersey Beat* office included the Beatles and Brian Epstein who reviewed records for the paper. During a Mersey Beat office move, a large bundle of John's stories and poems, written for the paper under his 'Beatcomber' pseudonym, managed to get 'lost'.

Another regular caller was Cavern DJ Bob Wooler who wrote a column called 'The Roving I'. The first article ever written about the Beatles was one penned by Bob for Mersey Beat in mid-1961. Needless to say, copies of *Mersey Beat* are now much sought after collectors' items.

Bill Harry is an authority on the Beatles. A prolific writer, he is the author of well over a score of books about them including *The Book of Lennon*, *The Beatles Who's Who*, and *The Beatles Encyclopedia*. Find out more on Bill's informative website and blog: *www.mersey-beat.net* and *billharry.co.uk/*

(Turn left into Bold Street.)

BOLD STREET (I) *(L1 4JA)*

On the right hand side, at number 89 (now Bold Street Coffee), near the top of the street, was the Odd Spot Club, venue for two Beatles gigs during 1962. John Dykins, partner of John's mother, Julia, was once a waiter here.

At No. 83, was Kaye Photography (now Bold Street Nails). When Brian Epstein needed new publicity photographs of the Beatles with the just-recruited Ringo he turned to one of Liverpool's best-known social photographers, Bill Connell, alias Peter Kaye. In those days Bill had a shop in Park Road and a modest studio in Newington, a shabby side street off Bold Street. Later he moved his operations to Bold Street, known in its heyday as 'The Bond Street of the North'. Those early historic images of the Beatles taken by Bill Connell and his young assistant Les Chadwick in their studio, at the Pier Head, on derelict sites in Liverpool's docklands, in the Cavern, and other Mersey Beat venues, can be seen in Peter Kaye's *Beatles in Liverpool*, largely put together by Bill's assistant, Margaret Roberts, and published in 1987. Sadly, Bill, a flamboyant, larger-than-life character, died the following year and Apple now owns the copyright of most of his photographs. See also p40 for another Bold Street Beatle landmark.

(Continue down Bold Street and turn left into Slater Street. Near its junction with Seel Street, is the Jacaranda Club. Also notice O'Brien's (then the Marlborough pub), another occasional watering hole during the Beatles' early years.)

JACARANDA CLUB *23 Slater Street (L1 4BW)*

Once owned by Allan Williams, the 'Jac' was a favourite place for the Beatles to hang out during their student days in the late 1950s. They would sit in the window playing their guitars, munching the Jac's famous bacon butties and making sarcastic remarks to the office girls coming in for a lunchtime snack. Downstairs, in the evening, the tiny airless basement reverberated to the then unlikely sound of the immensely popular 'Royal Caribbean' West Indian steel band. I can personally vouch that it was like the Black Hole of Calcutta, far sweatier than the Cavern!

The Beatles played about a dozen lunchtime and Monday evening engagements from May 1960 when the Royal Caribbean had their night off. Their payment? Coca Cola and beans on toast.

Also picture the scene on Tuesday, 15 August 1960 as the five Beatles, Allan Williams, his wife Beryl and her brother Barry Chang, and Allan's Caribbean friend 'Lord Woodbine', all crammed into Allan's battered old van and set off on their eventful journey to Hamburg.

The completely refurbished Jac reopened in 1996 with Pete and his Pete Best Band on stage. Pete commented – "It was in the Jacaranda that I first appeared with the Beatles, just before they went over to Germany – it would have been way back in August 1960. We were so poor in those days, we had our girlfriends sitting in the front with mike stands strapped to broom handles. But it was excellent. It was the place to be; everyone used to arrange to meet up at the Jac."

Basement murals, supposedly painted by John and Stu Sutcliffe during their art student days, were restored in time for the reopening. Mysteriously, the Jac closed its doors again in October 2011 but reopened three years later.

The original Jacaranda Club looked very different from the present one; it occupied half the frontage of the present Jac; this was the half adjacent to the Marlborough pub (renamed O'Brien's).

(Retrace your steps to Bold Street and turn left.)

Left: The Lyceum, showing Reece's Lyceum Café, photographed in 1974. Right: Bold Street in 1961, a time when the street was still dubbed 'The Bond Street of the north'. Even into the mid-60s you could buy a Rolls Royce or an antique here or shop for a mink coat at a choice of eleven furriers, and end your shopping spree with lunch at a gentleman's club.

Liverpool City Centre

BOLD STREET (2) *(L1 4DJ)*

At the bottom of Bold Street is the Lyceum, built about 1800, which once housed Reece's 'Lyceum Cafe', an old-fashioned Liverpool institution now sadly gone. The Beatles used to meet here for coffee and, it is said, pass the time composing songs on the backs of menus and table napkins. Other coffee bars frequented in this street included the Kardomah and El Cabala, the trendiest coffee bar in 60s Liverpool.

(At the bottom of Bold Street, look left to Hanover House, the building next to the bank)

EPSTEIN THEATRE (FORMERLY NEPTUNE THEATRE)
Hanover Street *(L1 3DZ)*

In August 1997, on the 30th anniversary of Brian Epstein's death, Liverpool City Council dedicated their theatre, previously called the Neptune Theatre, to his memory. Paul remarked – "Brian would have loved this, to have a theatre in his name. He was always very keen on acting." Actually, Brian once did buy a theatre of his very own...the *Saville* in London's Shaftesbury Avenue in April 1965. The Neptune Theatre 'sat' on top of Crane's music store which, along with Rushworth's and Hessy's, were the three most frequented by musicians in the 50s and 60s.

(Cross at the traffic lights into Church Street. The next street on the right is Parker Street.)

FORMER REECE'S RESTAURANT
Above Superdrug store, Parker Street/Leigh Street *(L1 1DJ)*

Reece's first floor restaurant was the unlikely venue for John and Cynthia's wedding breakfast on 23 August 1962. After their wedding in the Mount Pleasant Register Office, they dashed through the pouring rain with Paul, George and Brian in tow to fight for a table along with dozens of other lunchtime shoppers and office workers. The set lunch of soup, roast chicken and trifle was paid for by Brian. The newly-weds were toasted with water since the restaurant was not licensed to serve alcohol during the daytime.

(Continue along Church Street to School Lane, on the left. Facing you at the end of School Lane is Bluecoat Chambers.)

Left: the Crane Building (now renamed Hanover House), built 1913-15 as a music store. Designed by Walter Aubrey Thomas, whose most famous building is the Royal Liver Building, it also housed the Neptune Theatre (originally the Crane Theatre) which has been renamed the Epstein Theatre; Centre: another building by Thomas; this one housed the Reece's restaurant where John and Cynthia celebrated their wedding; Right: Bluecoat Chambers.

BLUECOAT CHAMBERS *School Lane (L1 3BX)*

Dating from 1717, this stunning Queen Anne period building, the oldest in Liverpool city centre, is the legacy of a Liverpool slave trader and do-gooder, Bryan Blundell... the city has always been a place of contradiction and controversy.

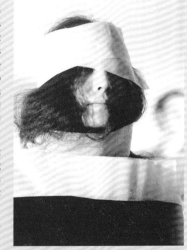

Long a centre for the arts, Yoko Ono appeared here on 26 September 1967 in a 'happening', a phenomenon of the 60s that seemed even dafter then than it does now. People sat dangling their legs over the stage eating sandwiches. The audience was invited to come on stage to chalk messages on a blackboard. And, as a climax, Yoko (pictured right) was bound to a chair with bandages and enveloped in smoke.

Less than a year earlier John had met Yoko for the first time at a private viewing of her avant-garde exhibition at London's Indica Gallery. Although he didn't know it at the time, he had met his soul mate.

In 1990 the Bluecoat staged an exhibition of works by Stuart Sutcliffe.

Following a radical £12.5m transformation, the complex reopened in March 2008 in time to celebrate the city's year as European Capital of Culture. Returning 41 years after her first ever paid performance was given at the Bluecoat, Yoko Ono gave a special one-hour live performance here the following month.

(Continue along Church Street to its junction with Paradise Street and Whitechapel. McDonald's has replaced Horne Brothers the gentlemen's outfitters in the basement of which was a barber shop where Brian Epstein sent the Beatles as part of his smarten up plan. Opposite, in Lord Street, was Times Furnishing where Brian served a six month sales apprenticeship for a weekly wage of £5 when he was 18 years old. Turn right into Whitechapel on the corner of which is the clothes store 'Forever 21' that has replaced the old NEMS building.

Stairway to fame. The Beatles pose between floors at NEMS, on 24 January 1963. Only Paul looks remotely animated with John, Ringo and George no doubt wishing they were someplace else. Eighteen days later they recorded, in just one day, their brilliant debut album, 'Please Please Me' which went to No. 1 in the UK charts.

FORMER NEMS RECORD SHOP & OFFICES

12-14 Whitechapel (L1 6DZ)

Following the success that Brian Epstein had made of the Great Charlotte Street branch of NEMS, his father handed him the task of expanding into a brand new development at 12-14 Whitechapel. This flagship NEMS store opened on 31 May 1960 with the actor and singer/songwriter Anthony Newley performing the ribbon cutting ceremony. Although the emphasis was on its two floors of records, the store's other floors also stocked a wide range of household electrical appliances including record players, televisions and radios. It was a runaway success and the teens of Merseyside flocked to it.

Legend has it that, on Saturday, 28 October 1961, 20-year old Raymond Jones, having heard the record *My Bonnie* by the Beatles, a scorching rocker, at Hambleton Hall played by DJ Bob Wooler, walked into NEMS record store and asked for it, without success.

Wooler had encouraged his youthful audience to ask for it at their record shops. Raymond Jones took his advice and asked Brian Epstein for the record at this store. Epstein prided himself on being able to search out any record asked for by his customers and tracked down the elusive record which turned out to be a minor best seller for him. Curious to find out more about the group that he claimed he'd never heard of before, he decided to visit the nearby Cavern club on 9 November 1961 when the Beatles were making one of their regular lunch-time appearances. The rest is history.

It has since been suggested that Epstein was fully aware of the Beatles' popularity months before Raymond Jones asked him for their record. Surely, it is argued, the astute Epstein could not have avoided seeing the prominent coverage given to them on the front covers of *Mersey Beat*, the newspaper for which he both wrote reviews and sold in his store, or the dance tickets for Beatles' shows sold by NEMS.

After decades of silence, Raymond Jones, by then living in Spain, resurfaced in 2010 to confirm that he was indeed the young man who had asked Brian Epstein for the

Beatles' *My Bonnie* record nearly forty years earlier. However, he says he first found out that the Beatles had made a record from a chance conversation with his sister's boyfriend, Kenny Johnson, guitarist with local group Mark Peters and the Cyclones.

The upstairs office here soon became the nerve centre for Brian's burgeoning NEMS Enterprises of which the Beatles were central. By the Summer of 1963 the meteoric growth of NEMS Enterprises had led to the office being re-located from here to first floor premises above the Wizard's Den joke shop at 24 Moorfields, a few streets away. In March of the following year Brian moved the entire NEMS Enterprises operation to London.

FORMER RUSHWORTH'S MUSIC HOUSE

Corner of Whitechapel/ Richmond Street *(L1 1HQ)*

Just a stone's throw away from NEMS, Rushworth's was the city's largest musical instrument suppliers and a Liverpool institution. Many of the Merseybeat groups, including the Beatles, bought their gear here. Their much-prized Gibson jumbo guitars were specially ordered by Rushworths from Gibson's factory at Kalamazoo, Michigan and formally presented to them on 10 September 1962. John always lamented that this, his favourite J-160E electro-acoustic jumbo, had been stolen in December the following year. The £160 guitar, used on some early Beatles recordings such as *Love Me Do* and *P.S. I Love You*, resurfaced in the late 60s and was eventually sold at auction in the USA in November 2015 for $2.41m (£1.6m).

Paul's dad bought him a trumpet from Rushworth's for his 14th birthday. Realising that he couldn't sing with a trumpet stuck in his mouth he soon swapped it for a £15 German Framus Zenith Model 17 acoustic guitar. He couldn't figure out how to play it...until he realised that the guitar was strung for right-handed players. He was a 'leftie'. Paul still has it in his guitar collection and can be seen with it on videos filmed in Los Angeles of *Early Days* from his 2014 album *New*.

Founded in 1831, the business, which in its heyday billed itself as the: 'Five Generation Music House – the largest in Europe', went bust in 2002 and the building is now home to a number of small businesses, including E. Rex Makin & Co. Solicitor Rex was Brian Epstein's friend, next door neighbour and advisor and relocated here from offices in the former NEMS Whitechapel building when it was demolished.

Left: the former Rushworths Music House, Whitechapel; Right: James Rushworth, company chairman, presents John and George with their new Gibson J-160 E electro-acoustic guitars.

Left: Hessy's Music Centre towards the end of its days in Stanley Street; Right: recreation of Hessy's shop front in the Beatles Story museum.

(Turn left into Stanley Street.)

FORMER HESSY'S *(Now Wongs Jewellers) 62 Stanley Street* (L1 6DS)

One of Liverpool's three major musical instrument stores during the Merseybeat years presided over by the ever-present Frank Hessy and his star salesman Jim Gretty. The price of buying a guitar included a three-chord 'lesson' from Jim, a club performer himself. It was Jim who had sold John his first 'proper' £15 guitar in 1957.

One early act of Brian Epstein as their manager was to clear the £200 debt which the Beatles owed Hessy's for John's Hofner Club 40 guitar, George's Futurama guitar and Paul's amplification equipment.

Hessy's later featured in the 1965 film *Ferry 'cross the Mersey* starring Gerry and the Pacemakers, other Merseybeat stars and disgraced disk jockey Jimmy Savile.

On the corner of the street, next door to Hessy's, which closed its doors for the last time in 1995, was the Kardomah Coffee House (now also part of Wongs) another Liverpool institution and non-alcoholic hangout for the Beatles.

(Continue up Stanley Street and cross the road to the Eleanor Rigby statue)

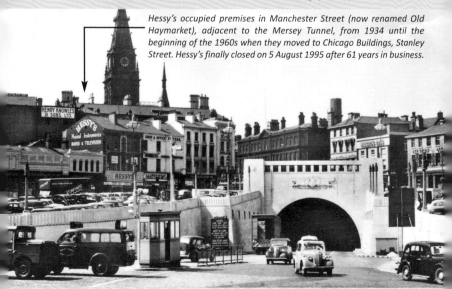

Hessy's occupied premises in Manchester Street (now renamed Old Haymarket), adjacent to the Mersey Tunnel, from 1934 until the beginning of the 1960s when they moved to Chicago Buildings, Stanley Street. Hessy's finally closed on 5 August 1995 after 61 years in business.

THE CAVERN QUARTER:

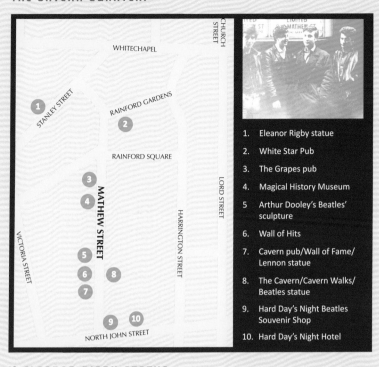

1. Eleanor Rigby statue
2. White Star Pub
3. The Grapes pub
4. Magical History Museum
5. Arthur Dooley's Beatles' sculpture
6. Wall of Hits
7. Cavern pub/Wall of Fame/Lennon statue
8. The Cavern/Cavern Walks/Beatles statue
9. Hard Day's Night Beatles Souvenir Shop
10. Hard Day's Night Hotel

1) ELEANOR RIGBY STATUE *Stanley Street (L1 6AL)*

Dedicated to 'all the lonely people'...the mythical, sad figure in the Beatles' famous song, was sculpted by Tommy *'I've never felt more like singing the blues'* Steele as a tribute to the Liverpudlian pop idols.

In the certain knowledge that the City Fathers would not put their hands in their pockets for any memorial to the Beatles, Tommy gave it to them for 'half a sixpence'* just over one penny in 'new money'. The £4,000 cost of casting the statue in bronze was met by the Liverpool Echo newspaper.

Almost as interesting as the statue itself is what Tommy enigmatically placed inside it: a four leaf clover for luck, a page from the Bible for spiritual help, a sonnet for lovers, an adventure book for excitement and a pair of football boots for action.

On 3 December 1982 the perky Cockney performed the official unveiling of his creation, explaining – "I put them all inside the statue so she would be full of magical properties. I give Eleanor to Liverpool with an open heart and many thanks for my happy times in the City". Tommy had another date with Eleanor in 2003 when he celebrated her 21st anniversary.

*An allusion to the 'Half a Sixpence' musical comedy show and film starring Tommy Steele.

(Retrace your steps and turn right into Mathew Street.)

MATHEW STREET *(L2 6RE)*

The Mathew Street you see today is nothing like the narrow, grubby little warehouse street of the Merseybeat era. Nowadays it is part of the trendy 'Cavern Quarter' pub and club scene and has well and truly cashed in on its Beatles heritage. The street was once home to Eric's the legendary 70s punk club associated with some of the biggest names of that era, such as Elvis Costello, the Clash and the Sex Pistols. Local groups who later made it big included Dead or Alive, Echo and the Bunnymen, The Teardrop Explodes and OMD.

(Look down Rainford Gardens to the White Star pub.)

2) WHITE STAR PUB *Rainford Gardens* *(L2 6PT)*

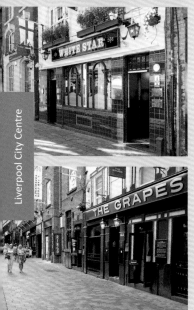

Mecca for drinkers of Draft Bass, the White Star (named after the Liverpool shipping line whose most famous liner was the ill-starred *Titanic*) was an alternative venue to the Grapes pub for the Beatles and the other groups appearing at the Cavern. *(Return to Mathew Street)*

3) THE GRAPES PUB

'The Beatles' Pub', as it is known, was opposite the Cavern and therefore the obvious choice for the Beatles and other Merseybeat groups. It was a popular refuge from the Cavern where coffee or Coca Cola were the strongest drinks on offer. Here the Beatles would down pints of Brown Mix or Black Velvet and Brian, when he did join them, decorously sipped brandy. When drummer Pete Best was sacked from the Beatles on 16 August 1962, he drowned his sorrows here with their Road Manager, Neil Aspinall. In the back room is a photograph of the Beatles, with Pete, in the exact place where they regularly sat: the original seat and wallpaper have been preserved.

4) MAGICAL HISTORY MUSEUM

This, the newest addition to Mathew Street, opened its doors in July 2018. In contrast to The Beatles Story 'museum' at Albert Dock, this exhibition is very much centered on Beatles' memorabilia, especially items from the collection of Pete Best and family, such as Pete's drum kit from the early 60s. There are medals worn by John

Lennon on the *Sgt Pepper* album artwork, George Harrison's Futurama Grazioso guitar and Paul McCartney's bass guitar speaker, besides clothing, letters, posters, jewellery, photographs and so much more, all exhibited on the museum's four floors.

5] ARTHUR DOOLEY'S BEATLES SCULPTURE

You'll either love or loathe this celebration of the Fab Four by local sculptor the late Arthur Dooley, a giant of a man with a larger-than-life character to match. When it was erected in 1974, this curious dedication to the 'Four Lads Who Shook The World' consisted of four cherubic images fashioned from plastic dolls. A guitar-carrying cherub complete with a 'Lennon Lives' halo was added in 1980.

6] WALL OF NUMBER 1 HITS

The 'Wall of Number 1 Hits' is a commemoration of the 57 No.1. hit records by Liverpool bands and artistes. They range from Lita Roza's 1953 hit *How Much is that Doggie in the Window?* to The Justice Collective's 2012 hit *He Ain't Heavy He's My Brother* and, of course, include the seventeen Beatles hits and eight No 1s by individual Beatles and Wings. The original 'Wall of Hits' was unveiled on 14 March, 2001, by 75 year old Lita Roza (1926-2008). What you see today (right) is its more recent replacement.

7] CAVERN PUB/WALL OF FAME/ LENNON STATUE

The 40th anniversary of the Cavern was celebrated on 16 January 1997. A 'Wall of Fame' formed of bricks etched with the names of the 1,800 plus bands who played the club between 1957 and 1973 was unveiled by Gerry Marsden of Gerry and the Pacemakers. At the same time Billy J Kramer unveiled a statue which, following a head transplant, bears some resemblance to John Lennon. The cosy subterranean Cavern Pub opened in 1994 and is themed around the bands and stars who played at the Cavern including the Rolling Stones, the Who, Chuck Berry, Jimi Hendrix and, of course, the Beatles. As well as being a pub it is also a mini 'museum' with interesting photographs adorning the walls and guitars in glass cases signed by famous musicians.

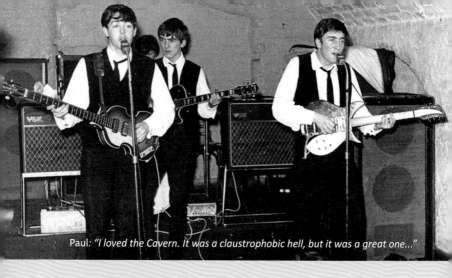

Paul: *"I loved the Cavern. It was a claustrophobic hell, but it was a great one..."*

8) THE CAVERNCLUB/CAVERN/WALKS/BEATLES STATUE

The stylish Cavern Walks complex opened in Spring 1984 and replaced a row of grimy old warehouses. In one of these, number ten, formerly a wine and spirit store, egg packing station and even a make-shift air raid shelter against Hitler's Luftwaffe, 18 stone steps led down to a cellar club the name of which was to become known the world over. That club was the Cavern.

Here, in the catacombed darkness beneath your feet, the Beatles played some 290 times. They made their debut during the lunchtime of Thursday, 9th February 1961 for £5 and went on to play a further 151 lunch-time sessions. Their final performance, for £300, took place on the evening of Saturday 3 August 1963. Along with other top local groups, for the Mersey Sound was never just the Beatles, they made the Cavern the most famous rock and roll venue of its day.

But the Cavern had not always echoed to the big beat sound. When doctor's son Alan Sytner bought it in 1956 he planned a similar venture to 'Le Caveau Francais', the Parisian jazz club. The Cavern first opened its doors to a jazz-only crowd on 16 January 1957, but soon yielded to the skiffle craze sweeping the country at that time. It was to be the thin end of a very large rock and roll wedge.

Indeed, it was as the Quarrymen skiffle group that the young Beatles made their first true appearance at the Cavern on Wednesday, 7 August 1957. Paul missed this historic event. He was away at a Boy Scout Summer camp at the time. And six months were to pass before the 14-year old George Harrison was to meet the Quarrymen for the first time. The original 1957 Quarrymen line-up (minus John Lennon and of course it wasn't the *real* Cavern) played their first gig at the Cavern almost 42 years to the day of their debut appearance.

Maggie May, Railroad Bill, Cumberland Gap and other Lonnie Donegan skiffle numbers would have been as much a part of the Beatles' repertoire in those days as their distinctive versions of Elvis, Chuck Berry and Buddy Holly classics. More significantly, by this time, the first hesitant efforts of the Lennon/McCartney song-writing partnership were also being given an airing.

48

The two men most associated with the Cavern Club: below left: DJ., promoter and punster Bob Wooler, and below right: Ray McFall, owner of the Cavern from 1959-1966. Right: display to the right of the main entrance door of 8 Mathew Street marking the site of the doorway to the original Cavern.

DON'T YOU ROCK ME DADDY-O

In late 1959 the Cavern passed into the hands of accountant Ray McFall. Although rock and roll had occasionally sneaked in, much to the disgust of the regular jazz purists, it was not until 25 May 1960 that McFall relented to allow the very first beat night. On stage that night were the immensely popular Cass and the Cassanovas (later the Big Three) and Rory Storm and the Hurricanes whose drummer was none other than Ringo Starr. From that night the Cavern was 'lost' to rock and roll.

Welcoming fans to 'the best of cellars', the Cavern's legendary DJ, Bob Wooler, the 'Prince of Pun', introduced the cream of the hundreds of Merseyside groups that had emerged out of the short-lived skiffle boom – the Searchers, the Swinging Blue Jeans, the Remo Four, Gerry and the Pacemakers, Billy J Kramer and the Dakotas, the Fourmost, the Big Three and, of course, the Beatles. And there was a girl singer, the Cavern's cloakroom attendant Priscilla White, better known as Cilla Black.

'LEGENDS IN THEIR OWN LUNCHTIME'

On Thursday, 9 November 1961, during one of its popular lunchtime sessions, a sober-suited 27-year old Brian Epstein visited the Cavern to see for himself its star performers, the Beatles. He watched. He listened. He was hooked. Despite the warnings of Allan Williams, their first manager, "not to touch them with a fucking barge-pole", Brian eventually signed them up in his NEMS office in nearby Whitechapel on Wednesday 24 January 1962. It was an auspicious, and busy day for the Beatles – they had also played lunchtime and evening sessions at the Cavern.

To say that the Beatles' stage persona at the time of Brian's first visit was 'informal' would be a gross under-statement. They would smoke cigarettes, drink tea and eat jam butties on stage, crack jokes, swear, and exchange banter with the audience. Brian would soon change all that.

CAVERN OF DREAMS

Amid howls of protest, the debt-ridden Cavern was closed down by the Official Receiver on 28 February 1966. It was ceremoniously re-opened five months later on 23 July by Labour Prime Minister Harold Wilson ('Pipe Smoker of the Year' in 1965) who was presented with a wooden pipe crafted from the original stage which had been broken up in 1964 and sold piece by piece for charity.

Although it survived for another seven years, it closed its doors for the last time on 27 May 1973 as Paul McCartney and his new group Wings played the final night of their UK tour at the Hammersmith Odeon Cinema. The warehouse was then bulldozed to provide a working site for the construction of the city's new underground railway system. Most Beatle fans remain amazed that the City of Liverpool did nothing to stop this act of cultural vandalism. Who can blame them?

For a number of years the historic Cavern site was an unsightly temporary car park before it was bought by the Liverpool-based company Royal Life (now Resolution) and redeveloped into the Cavern Walks shops and office complex you see today.

THE CAVERN LIVES!

Cavern Walks bristles with Beatle features. Cynthia Lennon designed the terra-cotta embellishments to its frontage. In the shopping mall look out for the much-derided 'official' statue to the Fab Four by John Doubleday (above) It was unveiled by Paul's brother, Mike McCartney who, nonplussed, asked… "Which one's our kid?!"

Most exciting of all, the Cavern club was rebuilt as near to the original as possible using bricks saved from the old Cavern. Whilst it is not an exact replica and can never recapture the atmosphere of the original Cavern, it is well worth a visit since it's the nearest thing to the real Cavern that you can experience. Another, smaller scale, replica can be found in the Beatles Story at Albert Dock.

One of the high spots for the 'new' Cavern came on 14 December 1999 when Paul performed his last gig of the millennium here in front of 150 lucky fans and a similar number of media people. Paul explained – "I am going back for just one night as a nod to the music that has and will ever thrill me. I can't think of a better way to rock out the end of the century than with a rock 'n' roll gig at the Cavern."

Another high spot came at 2pm on 26 July 2018 when Paul performed a 'secret' gig here. Fittingly, he began by saying "Liverpool! Cavern! These are words that go together well." Two hours and nearly thirty songs later, on one of the hottest days of the year the by now sweat-soaked sprightly 76 year-old had rolled back the years and delivered a stunning set covering pre-Beatles songs, Beatles and Wings classics and even songs from his new album *Egypt Station*. Concluding his review, the NME's

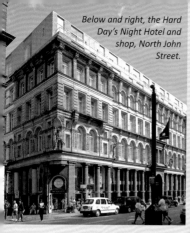

Below and right, the Hard Day's Night Hotel and shop, North John Street.

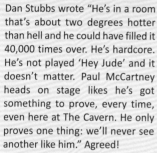

Dan Stubbs wrote "He's in a room that's about two degrees hotter than hell and he could have filled it 40,000 times over. He's hardcore. He's not played 'Hey Jude' and it doesn't matter. Paul McCartney heads on stage likes he's got something to prove, every time, even here at The Cavern. He only proves one thing: we'll never see another like him." Agreed!

9] HARD DAYS NIGHT SHOP *1, Mathew Street (L2 6RR)*

On the corner of Mathew Street and North John Street (pictured above) is the well-stocked Hard Day's Night Beatles shop which sells an extensive range of Apple-licensed Beatles gear.

10] HARD DAYS NIGHT HOTEL

Central Buildings, North John Street (L2 6RR) www.harddaysnighthotel.com

Whilst a Beatles-inspired hotel in Liverpool had been under discussion for many years, the Hard Days Night Hotel finally opened on 1 February 2008. This fab four-star 'boutique' hotel is ideally located in a beautiful restored Grade Two Listed building dating from 1884 on the corner of Mathew Street and North John Street, just yards away from the famous Cavern club, spiritual home of the Fab Four.

Each of the 110 bedrooms, including two suites named after Lennon and McCartney, is adorned with specially-commissioned artwork by internationally-acclaimed American artist Shannon.

The public areas of the hotel include Blakes Restaurant (named after Sir Peter Blake), Bar Four, the Live Lounge and The Lounge & Bar. There are also conference and event suites for private entertaining and corporate events – Beatles fans can even get married in the unique Wedding Suite.

The full-height statues of the individual Beatles perched above the polished granite columns of the Hard Days Night Hotel are, in this writer's view, bordering on the grotesque and spoil the elegant façade of this historic building.

John: *"As a kid I used to go to their garden parties with my friends Ivan, Nigel and Pete. We'd all go up there and hang out and sell lemonade bottles. We always had fun at Strawberry Field."*

South Liverpool

CITY CENTRE

EDGE HILL

DINGLE

TOXTETH

WAVERTREE

CHILDWALL

SEFTON PARK

CALDER-STONES PARK

AIGBURTH

ALLERTON

WOOLTON

GARSTON

SPEKE

RIVER MERSEY

WAVERTREE ROAD
UPPER PARLIAMENT STREET
WAPING
PRINCES ROAD
PARK ROAD
HIGH PARK STREET
SMITHDOWN ROAD
PICTON ROAD
CHILDWALL ROAD
ULLET ROAD
CHURCH ROAD
AIGBURTH DRIVE
QUEENS DRIVE
MOSSLEY HILL DRIVE
AIGBURTH ROAD
AIGBURTH HALL AVENUE
MATHER AVENUE
BOOKER AVENUE
ALLERTON ROAD
MATHER AVENUE
ST MARY'S ROAD
HORROCKS AVENUE
WOOLTON ROAD
SPEKE ROAD
SPEKE BOULEVARD
WOODEND AVENUE
WESTERN AVENUE
NORTH PARADE
MACKETS LANE
HALEWOOD ROAD
BELLE VALE ROAD
CHILDWALL VALLEY ROAD
GATEACRE BROW
BEACONSFIELD ROAD
MENLOVE AVENUE
ALLERTON ROAD
QUEENS DRIVE
CHURCH ROAD

SOUTH LIVERPOOL

1. 9 Madryn Street
2. 10 Admiral Grove
3. Empress Pub
4. St Silas School
5. Dingle Vale School
6. 37 Aigburth Drive
7. Sefton General
8. 93 Garmoyle Road
9. Penny Lane
11. Dovedale Rd School
12. 9 Newcastle Road
13. Mosspits Lne School
14. 12 Arnold Grove
15. 197 Queens Drive
16. 28 Hillside Road
17. Quarry Bank School
18. 72 Western Avenue
19. 251 Menlove Avenue
21. 174 Mackets Lane
22. 20 Forthlin Road
23. 1 Blomfield Road
24. Allerton Cemetery
25. Wilson Hall
26. 72 Western Avenue
27. Stockton Wd School
28. 25 Upton Green
29. 12 Ardwick Road

54

Here is a selection of some of the more important Beatle places outside the city centre but still within or near the Liverpool boundary. These are grouped under South Liverpool and North & East Liverpool.

The number after each of the addresses indicates the postal districts into which the city is divided and, in brackets, their post codes so that you can easily find them on your mobile device using, for example, Google maps.

All the places can be reached by public transport; use the Merseytravel Journey Planner ap for mobile devices or log on to www.merseytravel.gov.uk; 'phone the Merseytravel Line on 0151 236 7676 seven days a week (7am to 8pm Mon-Fri; 8am-8pm weekends and Bank Holidays) or visit the Queen Square Travel Centre or Liverpool One Bus Station.

'RINGOLAND' – THE DINGLE

John: *"Ringo was the only real city kid...I think he came out of the lousiest area. He doesn't care, he probably had more fun there."*

9 MADRYN STREET — RINGO'S BIRTHPLACE

off High Park Street, Dingle, Liverpool 8 (L8 3TT)

Humble birthplace of the eldest Beatle. Richard ('Richy') Starkey, alias Ringo Starr, was born in an upstairs bedroom of this Victorian terraced house on 7 July 1940, a month before Hitler started his bombing raids on the nearby docks.

Ringo was just three when his mother Elsie and father, also Richard (Big Richy, Little Richy), split up after seven years of marriage. To make ends meet, Elsie worked, among other things, as a part-time barmaid, leaving young Ringo either with neighbours or more often than not with Grandma and Grandad Starkey who lived at the very end of the street at No. 59 (pictured below right). Curiously, this is where Ringo's father moved to after

South Liverpool

2016 – Ringo's birthplace, his grandparents' house (extreme right), and all the other houses in Madryn Street, boarded up and awaiting the regeneration of the 'Welsh Streets' area that began in 2017.

Left: number 9 Madryn Street, humble 'two up, two down' abode of Richard Starkey a.k.a. Richy/Ringo Starr; Centre: Ringo sings about Madryn Street and Admiral Grove on his 'Liverpool 8" album; Right: Ringo pictured by Liverpool photographer Peter Kaye.

his marriage to Elsie failed. Grandad Starkey, a boilerman who worked at the docks, once made Ringo a big train 'with a real fire in the engine' which not surprisingly was the talk of the street. Fitting then that much later in life Ringo should be so closely associated with the ever-popular 'Thomas the Tank Engine' stories for which he did the voice-over.

Partly because the rent was cheaper, partly to avoid bumping into Big Richy, but mainly to help an old friend who had a husband and three children, Elsie swapped her house for her friend's even smaller house in nearby Admiral Grove. Six-year old Ringo made the short house move perched on the back of a handcart.

"Our neighbourhood was really bombed. We had to hide a lot, I've been told since; we used to hide in the coal cellar (it was like a cupboard). I remember big gaps in the streets where houses stood. We used to play on the rubble when I was older, and in the air-raid shelters." Ringo.

After many years of dereliction and abandonment, Ringo's birthplace was sold at a Tokyo auction in March 1997 for £13,250. Although subsequently renovated it remained abandoned and boarded-up for years. In September 2005, Liverpool City Council perversely decided that Madryn Street, along with ten other neighbouring Victorian streets (the so-called 'Welsh Streets'), should be bulldozed. In a partial reprieve, the Council curiously pledged that, although Ringo's birthplace had no historical significance, it would be dismantled brick by brick and stored safely away until it could finally be decided where it could be re-built. This, from the same City Council that 50 years previously removed the magnificent sculpture above the south pediment of St George's Hall temporarily on safety grounds, put it into storage...and then 'lost' it – they 'think' it ended up as hardcore! A similarly flawed plan to reconstruct 9 Madryn Street in the Museum of Liverpool was also thankfully abandoned. As a result of campaigning by SAVE Britain's Heritage, the City Council finally agreed in February 2016 that this house and hundreds of others in the 'Welsh Streets', would be saved and the whole area regenerated. Unlike many Liverpudlians who are unable to find affordable housing, Ringo, who was born and brought up here in the 'slums of Liverpool', doesn't have a housing problem; nowadays, he divides his time between his main home in Los Angeles and one in London. Work began in 2017 and continues.

Ringo paid his own special tribute to Madryn Street and Liverpool on his 2008 Album 'Liverpool 8'. The lead track takes its name from the album title ..."Liverpool I left you, said goodbye to Madryn Street." Look for the terrific Parlophone video (Ringo Starr – Liverpool 8) on YouTube.

No. 10 Admiral Grove, the pink and white house in this neat Victorian row of terraced houses, is a place of pilgrimage for Ringo's many fans. It was bought in April 2016 by a private buyer who already owns two other Beatle-associated homes: 1 Blomfield Road and 25 Upton Green.

10 ADMIRAL GROVE — RINGO'S HOUSE

off High Park Street, Liverpool (L8 8BH)

Ringo's tiny 'two up, two down' (two rooms upstairs, two rooms downstairs) home from the age of six until fame and fortune beyond his wildest imaginings were heaped on his humble shoulders after just six months as the Beatles' new drummer. Ever since, it seems to me, Ringo has had that permanent "How did all these wonderful things happen to an 'ordinary' little boy from Liverpool like me?" look about him.

Ringo's mother re-married in April 1954 when he was nearly 14. Her new husband, whom she had known for many years, was a Londoner called Harry Graves. After the war and an illness, he had come to Liverpool to take up a place on a Government training scheme for painters and decorators and, amazingly, 'for a beneficial change of air'. Remember, in those pre-Clean Air Act days, Liverpool had a well-deserved reputation for being one of the most air-polluted and soot-blackened cities in Britain, a place where lung-searing smogs were common.

The irony was compounded that same year when Ringo caught a cold which developed into pleurisy and then tuberculosis (TB). He was sent to convalesce at the Children's Hospital at Heswall on the healthy Wirral coast. He remained there for six months...and became the drummer in the ward band.

To Elsie's joy, Ringo and Harry hit it off from the start. Unwittingly, it was Harry who probably sparked off Ringo's fascination for all things American including a thwarted teenage attempt to emigrate to Texas. Harry was a painter at the giant United States Air Force base at Burtonwood near Liverpool and he often brought home the genuine American 'DC' comics, film magazines, candy and gum much prized by Liverpool children who usually had to make do with inferior English substitutes. He was also a very good singer and the 'star turn' at family parties.

When he left school at 15 having missed so much of his education through illness, Ringo became, in rapid succession, a British Rail messenger boy, a steward on the cruise boat *St. Tudno* that once sailed between Liverpool and Llandudno and an apprentice fitter with local firm, H. Hunt and Son. Also at Hunt's was his next door neighbour Ed Miles. During the skiffle craze Ringo joined his Eddie Clayton Skiffle Group.

When he was 20, and by then drummer with the hugely popular Merseybeat group Rory Storm and the Hurricanes, Ringo packed in his apprenticeship at Hunt's and

set off with the band to enter the big time...a 13-week season at Butlins Holiday Camp in Pwllheli, North Wales. It was here that he first became known as Ringo Starr and even had his own 'Starr-Time' solo spot with the group. I remember Rory telling me at the time that he thought Ringo had made a mistake leaving the Hurricanes because..."He won't get a 'Starr-Time' spot with the Beatles"!

The following Summer, Ringo celebrated his 21st birthday with a party at 10 Admiral Grove. Difficult though it is to believe, about 60 people crammed into this tiny house, including Cilla Black, Gerry and the Pacemakers and the Big Three.

On 30 August 1963 all four Beatles were here for the filming of footage for 'The Mersey Sound', a 29-minute documentary that can be seen on YouTube. John and Paul took a back seat on this occasion whilst Ringo was filmed emerging through the front door, fighting his way past hordes of small kids and getting into George's open-top car.

Elsie and Harry clung onto their home in the Dingle until 1965 when fan fever became just too much. However, unlike the other Beatle parents, they insisted on staying in Liverpool so Ringo bought them a luxurious bungalow in Woolton, a select area of the city, where they spent their remaining years.

THE EMPRESS PUBLIC HOUSE

High Park Street/Admiral Grove, Liverpool (L8 3UF)

To Beatle fans who own Ringo's first solo album *Sentimental Journey*, this typical Liverpool street corner pub will look familiar. He used a photograph of it on the front cover; the people in the windows are members of his family. The back cover features the former grocer's shop on the corner of Kinmel Street (opposite The Empress pub).

ST. SILAS CHURCH OF ENGLAND PRIMARY SCHOOL – RINGO'S FIRST SCHOOL **High Park Street, Liverpool (L8 3UQ)**

Ringo was just five years old when he began his primary school education here, although the modern school you see now replaced the original Victorian school he attended. Next door was the site of St Silas church where Ringo had been christened and which was a victim of a German air raid. He got off to a shaky start; on his very first day he came home for lunch at mid-day and told his mother that he didn't have to go back that day. She believed him...until she spotted all the other kids returning to school! He hated school from the word go and continued so until he left to move to the 'big school', aged eleven.

When he was almost seven his education suffered a serious setback. An attack of appendicitis worsened into peritonitis forcing him to spend a year away from school. Luckily, he had a close childhood friend, Marie Maguire, who helped him to catch up. Now Marie Crawford she is, appropriately, an official BeatleGuide as well as Godmother to Zak, Ringo and Maureen's first child.

In 1999 Ringo made a donation to his old school to help create an activity centre for the pupils.

DINGLE VALE SECONDARY MODERN — RINGO'S SECONDARY SCHOOL *(now University Academy) Dingle Vale, Liverpool (L8 9SJ)*

Ringo's school, from the ages of 11 to 15, although the final two years were again spent in hospital or at home. Not surprisingly, he left without any qualifications.

When he asked for an end-of-school report for use as a reference in his search for a job, he claimed that it was so long since he'd last been there that nobody could remember him. Ironically, when Ringo hit the big time, the school dragged out 'his' desk at one of their open days and charged visitors for the privilege of sitting in it. Ringo hated the school dinners here and opted for a Hovis loaf with the middle scooped out and stuffed with chips. Nowadays, Ringo is a drugs-free, non-smoking, non-drinking, healthy-eating, keep fit fanatic who 'found God' again at the age of 69.

SEFTON PARK AREA

37 AIGBURTH DRIVE (SEFTON PARK HOTEL) — STUART SUTCLIFFE'S HOME

Sefton Park, Liverpool *(L17 4JE)*

Stu Sutcliffe, who preceded Paul McCartney as the Beatles' bass player, lived in Flat 1 in this handsome Victorian villa overlooking Sefton Park lake. Stu was born in Edinburgh on 23 June 1940 but the Sutcliffe family subsequently moved to Huyton on the outskirts of Liverpool. He was already showing great artistic promise as a student at the Liverpool College of Art when he left the family flat here to move to 7 Percy Street near the college.

After his second trip to Hamburg with the Beatles, Stu decided to stay there with his German photographer girlfriend, Astrid Kerchherr, and study under Eduardo Paolozzi at the State Art College in the city. The following year, on 10 April 1962, he died of a cerebral haemorrhage in Astrid's arms as an ambulance sped them to hospital. Ironically, National Museums Liverpool has in its collection a letter sent to Stu's mother, Millie, from the consultant surgeon at Liverpool's Smithdown General Hospital who was handling his case. Stu had failed to turn up for an x-ray but the consultant didn't seemed concerned. His impression was that Stu's symptoms were simply of a nervous origin. Seven months later Stu was dead.

As children, each of the Beatles would have played in Sefton Park, the biggest and most popular of Liverpool's grand Victorian parks. George had a passionate interest in gardening and made a substantial donation towards the restoration of the Palm House, below left. Sefton Park boating lake, below right, was where John's mother Julia first met Freddie, his father.

SEFTON GENERAL HOSPITAL — JULIAN LENNON'S BIRTHPLACE

now Sefton Park Medical Centre and Asda supermarket, Smithdown Road, Liverpool (L15 2LQ)

Birthplace, on Monday 8 April 1963, of John Charles Julian Lennon – John after his famous father, Charles after Cynthia's father and Julian, the nearest they could get to John's mother Julia. However, apart from two small units – Smithdown Minor Injuries Centre for Children and Sefton Park Medical Centre – very little remains to remind us that this was once a large hospital. Most of the site is now taken up by an Asda supermarket.

The umbilical cord had been coiled around Julian's neck and when he made his grand entrance he was, to quote his mother, 'an awful yellow colour'. John missed all the drama; he was on tour in the South of England at the time. Two days later he was back on Merseyside playing the Majestic Ballroom in Birkenhead and saw his new son for the first time.

"Who's going to be a famous little rocker like his dad then?", John would prophetically ask the gurgling infant cradled in his arms. His visits to see Julian and Cynthia created enormous interest among staff and patients eager to catch a glimpse of the by now famous Beatle father.

But this hospital held bittersweet memories for John. Five years earlier he had rushed here by taxi to be given the devastating news that his beloved mother Julia had died following a road accident. Coincidentally, Julia's common law husband, John Dykins, also died here after being involved in a traffic accident in 1966. Their two daughters, John's half-sisters Julia and Jacqui Dykins, were also born here.

93 GARMOYLE ROAD — CYNTHIA LENNON'S FLAT

off Smithdown Road, Liverpool (L15 3JH)

John's art school girlfriend, Cynthia Powell, and Paul's girlfriend, Dot Rhone, both rented adjacent first floor rooms in this large Victorian terraced house for a short time in 1962. It has two claims to fame. Paul McCartney, who had bought engagement rings for Dot and himself, ended their relationship abruptly here one night after going out with her for nearly three years. And Julian Lennon was conceived here.

Dot had first met Paul in 1959 as an innocent 16-year old virgin; months later with Paul still a 17 year-old schoolboy, she fell pregnant. Some three months later she lost the baby. Now off the hook, Paul must have breathed a huge sigh of relief: in those pre-birth control pill days, a schoolboy fathering a child carried with it an unacceptable stigma.

In the summer of 1962 Cynthia found herself in the same situation. When she broke the news of her pregnancy to John he was horrified but, as was the fashion in those days, he readily agreed to 'do the right thing'…"There's only one thing for it Cyn, we'll have to get married." So they did.

Former Barclays Bank

Former Martins Bank

The barber she

"*Penny Lane is in my ears and in my eyes...*"

PENNY LANE AREA

PENNY LANE *Liverpool (L18 2DG)*

Here it is! The 'street' made famous in the Beatles' masterpiece *Penny Lane*. The shelter in the middle of the roundabout, the barber shop, the bank...they are all here, sometimes even beneath blue suburban skies.

The 'shelter in the middle of the roundabout' today bears little resemblance to the original single-storey tram and bus shelter of the Beatles' boyhoods. It was acquired in the late 1980s by an entrepreneur who converted it into 'Sgt Pepper's Bistro' but, for much of the time since then, it has sat empty and neglected.

There are *three* banks here or, to be precise, two former banks plus one still in business, the TSB bank. The former Barclays Bank is now the Penny Lane Hotel and the former Martins Bank is the Penny Lane Surgery. None of the places mentioned in the Beatles' song is actually in Penny Lane. They are all in Smithdown Place. However, this 'hub' has long been known as the Penny Lane roundabout.

If you stand here long enough, you may see a banker who never wears a mac or even a pretty nurse selling poppies from a tray. However, you will probably stand a better chance of seeing a fireman with his clean machine; perhaps he'll even have an hourglass and a picture of the Queen. The local fire station is only a short distance along Allerton Road/Mather Avenue.

Although Penny Lane was mainly a Paul song, John contributed some lyrics, explaining that he was re-living his childhood. For the first five years of his life he lived in Newcastle Road, just around the corner from Penny Lane. Daily for another six years he walked past the Penny Lane roundabout to and from school. As a mischievous boy he rode on the bumpers of tramcars and did some petty thieving from shops in the Penny Lane area. Later, with the Quarrymen, he played gigs at St Barnabas Church Hall in Penny Lane. Penny Lane was very much 'in his eyes and in his ears'.

The same was true of George. From the age of five until he passed the 'Eleven Plus' examination at eleven and went to Liverpool Institute High School, he would daily trudge up and down past Penny Lane on his way to and from Dovedale Road School.

As an art student, Cynthia whiled away the summer holidays serving behind the cosmetics counter of the Woolworths store here, now a Tesco Express and Costa coffee shop. On one occasion when she was shopping in Penny Lane she was gripped by labour pains...Julian Lennon was about to make his entrance into the world.

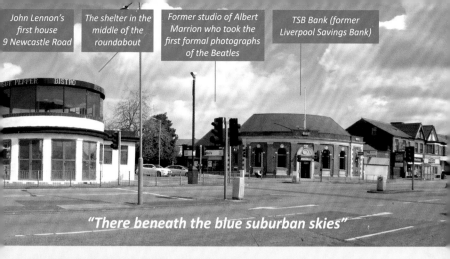

John Lennon's first house 9 Newcastle Road

The shelter in the middle of the roundabout

Former studio of Albert Marrion who took the first formal photographs of the Beatles

TSB Bank (former Liverpool Savings Bank)

"There beneath the blue suburban skies"

ST. BARNABAS CHURCH & CHURCH HALL *Penny Lane, Liverpool*

(L18 1LZ)

At St. Barnabas Church on 29 May 1982, Paul's brother Mike, formerly Mike McGear of The Scaffold, married the lovely Rowena Horne. Paul, who had once been a choirboy at St Barnabas, was the best man. The church is directly opposite the 'Penny Lane Roundabout'

Although St. Barnabas Church is situated in Penny Lane, St Barnabas Church Hall, now called *Dovedale Towers* and no longer connected with the church, is half way down Penny Lane at its junction with Dovedale Road. The Quarrymen played at "Barny's" as an interval skiffle group at Saturday night dances in the late 1950s.

Opposite Dovedale Towers is the Penny Lane chip shop ("Penny Lane is in my eyes, a four of fish and finger pies") and the Penny Lane Cakes shop.

The between-the-wars photograph below shows St Barnabas Church and part of the Penny Lane roundabout. A Liverpool Corporation tram heads for the Pier Head. To the right of the centre of the image is Penny Lane itself. Inset: Dovedale Towers, formerly St Barnabas Church Hall, is half-way up Penny Lane on the left. John, George, and to a lesser extent, Paul's formative years were steeped in the Penny Lane area.

South Liverpool

George: *"I have three recollections of Dovedale Road Infants School: the smell of boiled cabbage, a little girl who had blond curly hair and a Peter Pan house in the corner of the room, made by all the kids."* Right: John as a seven-year old at Dovedale Road.

DOVEDALE ROAD JUNIOR SCHOOL — JOHN AND GEORGE'S INFANT AND JUNIOR SCHOOL *off Penny Lane, Liverpool (L18 1JX)*

John first enrolled at Dovedale Road Infants School here on 6 May 1946. The 'Literary Lennon' quickly emerged and soon he was reading and writing fluently. Although he was inspired by books such as *Alice in Wonderland*, *Wind in the Willows* and *Just William*, John was an original thinker – "He won't do anything stereotyped" said his Headmaster. Even at that early age John himself recognised that somehow he was 'different' from the other kids.

He was just seven when he wrote his first 'book' – *Sport, Speed and Illustrated*. It saw the emergence of his distinctive style of jokes, drawings and stories alongside pasted-in images of film stars and footballers. Indeed, the sleeve of John's *Walls and Bridges* album features paintings of footballers and Red Indians done by him in his final term here in June 1952 when he was 11 years old.

John transferred to the Junior Boys School here in 1948 and finally left Dovedale for Quarry Bank Grammar School after he'd passed his '11-plus' exam in 1952. Although he didn't know it at the time, there was another younger little boy with latent musical talents at Dovedale at the same time as John. His name was George Harrison. He had been here since he was five, finally leaving when he was eleven to join Paul at the Liverpool Institute High School for Boys.

John enjoyed the six years he spent at this school and brought Yoko here when he first took her on a tour of his old Liverpool haunts. Later, Yoko made a number of donations to help pay for a new playground and equipment and visited the school in July 2001 and again in September 2010.

Other pupils who had made their mark include comedian Jimmy Tarbuck, broadcast journalist Peter Sissons and science fiction author Clive Barker.

9 NEWCASTLE ROAD — JOHN'S FIRST HOME *Liverpool (L15 9HP)*

Just around the corner from Penny Lane, this is the house where John was most likely conceived and where he mostly lived from the time he was a few days old until March 1946 when he and his mother left to live in a cramped one-bed flat with her 'new' lover, Bobby Dykins. Horrified by the unnatural three-in-a-bed living

John (1979): *"That's the underline first place I remember (Newcastle Road). It's a good way to start – red brick; front room never used, always curtains drawn, picture of a horse and carriage on the wall. There were only three bedrooms upstairs, one on the front of the street, one in the back, and one teeny little room in the middle."*

arrangements, Aunt Mimi alerted social services resulting in John being placed in the care of her and her husband George at Mendips. It was to be a long-term arrangement ending only when John left in January 1960 to move to 3 Gambier Terrace to share a flat with fellow art school students Stu Sutcliffe and Rod Davies.

9 Newcastle Road was the family home of George ('Pop') and Annie Stanley and their five daughters. The youngest was John's mother, Julia. A petite, vivacious red head, she was also spirited, fun-loving, musical and unconventional.

She married Liverpudlian Freddie Lennon, a ship's waiter in the Merchant Navy, on 3 December 1938. They spent their 'honeymoon' at the Trocadero Cinema in London Road; at the end of the film Julia returned here and Freddie went back to his lodgings, sailing off the next day on a three-month trip to the West Indies. John's contact with his father was sporadic and short-lived.

Julia worked as a barmaid at the large Tudor-style Brookhouse pub on Smithdown Road, fifteen minutes' walk from Newcastle Road. A wartime affair with Welsh soldier 'Taffy' Williams resulted in another baby which she immediately arranged to have adopted. After the war, Julia lived here for a time with her new man, John 'Bobby' Dykins (John cruelly nicknamed him 'Twitchy') whom she'd met whilst working at another pub, the Coffee House in Church Road North, Wavertree.

28 HILLSIDE ROAD— HOME OF MAL EVANS, BEATLES' ROAD MANAGER, PERSONAL ASSISTANT & FRIEND *Liverpool (L18 2ED)*

'Big Mal' was a part-time bouncer at the Cavern and Post Office engineer living here when he befriended the Beatles. He began working for them as assistant road manager and stayed with them until they broke up in 1970. During that time he travelled the world as their 'roadie', p.a. and bodyguard; he even appeared in four of the Beatles' five films and helped out on numerous recordings. All four Beatles were regular callers here. Sometimes Mal would bring stars appearing at the Liverpool Empire back for an after-show celebration. In those days you could have bumped into the likes of Diana Ross and the Supremes or the Beach Boys to name just two groups who chilled out here. Mal died in Los Angeles in 1976 following a face-off with police officers. Like John Lennon, Mal was shot dead aged 40 in the USA.

ENGLISH HERITAGE

MAL EVANS
1935 - 1976
Road Manager to
The Beatles
lived here

MOSSPITS LANE PRIMARY SCHOOL – JOHN'S FIRST SCHOOL

Mosspits Lane, Liverpool (L15 6UN)

This was the very first school attended by John. He enrolled here on 12 November 1945 and the school's Admission Book shows his address as 9 Newcastle Road and his parent/guardian as his father Alfred. Julia would take John to and from school which was just a seven-minute walk away from home. He remained here for no longer than six months since, by 6 May 1946, he was living with his Aunt Mimi and she had transferred him to Dovedale Road Infants School near Penny Lane.

Birthplace of George Harrison, at 12:10 a.m. on Thursday, 25 February, 1943.

South Liverpool

12 ARNOLD GROVE — GEORGE'S BIRTHPLACE

Wavertree, Liverpool (L15 8HP)

The upstairs front bedroom (pictured on the page opposite) was the birthplace on 25 February 1943 of the youngest Beatle, George Harrison. He lived in this cramped little house with an outside lavatory (rent 50 pence a week) for nearly seven years with his sister Louise, brothers Harold and Peter and mother and father, Louise and Harold. As George later recalled - "Our house was very small. Two up and two down – straight in off the pavement, step right out of the back room. The front room was never used. It had the posh lino and a three-piece suite and was freezing cold and nobody ever went in it. We'd all be huddled together in the kitchen, where the fire was, with the kettle on, and a little iron cooking stove."

When George was five he enrolled at Dovedale Road Primary School. His elder brother Peter was already there, in the same class as John Lennon.

George's mother and father, a bus driver and former steward on White Star liners sailing from the Pier Head, had been on the housing waiting list for 18 years when they finally got the news that they'd been allocated a brand new Council house at 25 Upton Green, Speke. They packed up all their belongings and left here on New Year's Day 1950.

George was christened (as 'Georgius Harrison' according to the baptism record which is in Latin) in Our Lady of Good Help Roman Catholic church, in nearby Chestnut Grove (since demolished). His maternal grandmother lived in the next street to George at 9 Albert Grove and he recalled running through the 'jigger' or 'back entry' to visit her.

South Liverpool

George: "Arnold Grove was a bit like Coronation Street...It was behind the Lamb Hotel in Wavertree. There was a big art-deco cinema there called the Abbey, and the Picton clock tower. Down a little cobbled lane was the slaughterhouse, where they used to shoot horses."

This is the Epstein family's attractive suburban villa. Harry Epstein had married Malka 'Minnie' Hymans, ten years his junior, in 1933; Brian came along in 1934, followed by brother Clive nearly two years later. Known as 'Queenie', Brian's houseproud mother was very much the queen bee, presiding over this commodious home with its five bedrooms, two bathrooms, kitchen, drawing room, dining room and library. Pictured above are Clive, Queenie and Brian at home in 1945 – she died in 1996, aged 82, having buried her husband and both sons.

197 QUEEN'S DRIVE — BRIAN EPSTEIN'S HOUSE Liverpool (L15 6XU)

This is the comfortable home in one of the city's more affluent suburbs into which Brian Epstein was born in 1934. His parents, Harry and Queenie, had moved into their new five-bedroomed detached house shortly after they married the previous year.

The Epstein family had run a furniture store in Liverpool's Walton Road since the beginning of the century. When he left school in 1950, virtually an academic failure, Brian reluctantly joined the family business. Although he had set his heart on becoming an actor, and had even studied for a time at the Royal Academy of Dramatic Art (RADA), it was not to be. Eventually, he channelled his energy and artistic talent into the family furniture and record stores with remarkable success.

To mark Paul's 21st birthday on 18 June 1963, Brian and his family hosted a morning cocktail party in the lounge of this house. Later that same day at another party held for Paul at his Aunty Jin's house at 147 Dinas Lane, Huyton, John beat up Cavern DJ Bob Wooler for insinuating that he was having a homosexual affair with Brian.

John, who lived not too far away from here, was a regular visitor, sitting with Brian in the morning room as they planned the Beatles' career.

QUARRY BANK, JOHN'S GRAMMAR SCHOOL
Now Calderstones School, Harthill Road, Liverpool (L18 3HS)

Almost from 4 September 1952, the day he first entered the Tudor-style Quarry Bank, formerly a mansion built by a local timber merchant, John was to be the bane of his teachers' lives and the despair of his Aunt Mimi. End of term school reports provide the clue – "Hopeless. Rather a clown in class. A shocking report. He is just wasting other pupils' time. Certainly on the road to failure."

His best subject was class anarchy of which he was the undisputed leader. Fighting,

South Liverpool

John: "The Quarrymen is the name of the group before it turned into the Beatles. The original group was named after my school, which was Quarry Bank and had a Latin motto which meant 'out of this rock' (that's symbolic) 'you will find truth." John is in the centre of the group below.

Quarry Bank old school building: the school hall where John and his Quarrymen skiffle group played some of their first gigs is to the left. Today, called 'Calderstones School', it is a specialist science college.

smoking 'loosies' (cigarettes bought in one's and two's by those who couldn't afford a full packet), disrupting classes, canings, refusing to conform and even being banned from school, were the tarnished hallmarks of an undistinguished five-year academic career at Quarry Bank. He left on 24 July 1957 after failing all his O Level examinations, even in his favourite subject, art.

Paradoxically, his Quarry Bank days were creatively, if not academically, productive. School exercise books were filled with highly original and hilariously funny stories, poems, drawings and cartoons. One called the *Daily Howl* which mercilessly parodied his teachers was passed under the desks from one giggling schoolboy to the next. A weather report read – 'Tomorrow will be Muggy followed by Tuggy, Wuggy and Thuggy.' A cartoon showed a blind man with glasses leading a blind dog, also with glasses; the physically afflicted were frequently the butt of his humour. This early work was to form the basis for his acclaimed books *In His Own Write* and *A Spaniard in the Works*.

It was also at Quarry Bank that John formed his first band, the Quarrymen, who were in essence a skiffle group made up of his classroom cronies. John had fronted the Quarrymen at a number of school dance held here.

Like his predecessor, John's headmaster, Mr Pobjoy, failed to 'knock him into shape' but John did credit him for getting him into art college. So, it was a case of 'Goodbye Quarry Bank and hello Liverpool College of Art' and the bohemian life of an art student.

STRAWBERRY FIELD *Beaconsfield Road, Liverpool (L25 6EJ)*

A short distance up the hill on the right hand side, look out for the old sandstone gate pillars inscribed 'Strawberry Field', the ornate strawberry coloured gates and the closed-off pathway leading to...'Strawberry Fields Forever'. Just stand there quietly and soak up the atmosphere of the place that inspired John Lennon to write his haunting masterpiece of pop imagery, the song that he considered was his greatest accomplishment.

Opened as a Salvation Army Children's Home in 1936, Strawberry Field was a large Victorian mansion set in extensive grounds. It was demolished in the late 60s and the land at the rear sold off to help pay for the newer buildings you see today.

Often as a young boy, John would come here with his Aunt Mimi to join in the fun of the Summer Fete. As the leader of his small gang of friends, he would avoid the

'cocky watchman' and clamber over the boundary wall to play and get up to mischief in the wooded grounds. It clearly held a special place in his heart. His association with Strawberry Field was a long one and lasted until the home's closure. He made a donation to the appeal for the new annexe, named Lennon Court when it opened in 1979. As part of their Liverpool 'pilgrimage', Yoko and Sean visited Strawberry Field in January, 1984, to meet the staff and children.

On 9th October that year, John's birthday, a parcel arrived from Yoko. It contained a cheque for $90,000, three records, a photograph and a special poem by Yoko.

Through a gift of $1m from Yoko, a 'twin' Strawberry Fields was created in 1985 from a neglected tear-shaped section of Central Park, New York – John and Yoko lived nearby in the Dakota Building on Central Park West/W 72nd St. It is a building that would not look out of place in Liverpool city centre's business district.

On 9 October 1998 the Lord Mayor of Liverpool was in New York helping Yoko to plant an oak tree there in John's honour. Yoko also collected the Freedom of the City of Liverpool scroll awarded posthumously to John in 1984. Coincidentally, Britain's first public park, designed by the great British landscape architect Joseph Paxton, at Birkenhead, across the river from Liverpool, was used as the model by the American parks pioneer Frederick Olmstead to create New York's Central Park.

Beatle fans worldwide were horrified when, in May 2000, thieves made off with the gates in broad daylight. The police were alerted and the gates were soon recovered – they had found their way into the hands of a scrap metal dealer who had bought them in good faith only later to hear media reports of their significance. Amidst fears that they might be stolen again, they were replaced by a pair of replica gates. The originals were refurbished and put into storage.

Sadly for Strawberry Field, times changed and the trend had increasingly been for children to be cared for in foster homes rather than institutions. On 31 May 2005, the inevitable happened and the gates to the world-famous children's home were finally closed...but hopefully, not forever.

On the 17 February 2017, the 50th anniversary of the release in the UK of the Beatles' iconic double-A single, Strawberry Fields / Penny Lane, the Salvation Army launched an appeal for funds to create a training and work placement hub for young people with learning disabilities. Also planned is an exhibition about the place, the song and John Lennon's early life around Strawberry Field. It looks hopeful that Strawberry Field as an important place of Beatles heritage and pilgrimage will be enhanced and continue into the future. (www.strawberryfieldliverpool.com)

MENDIPS, 251 MENLOVE AVENUE — JOHN LENNON'S HOUSE

Liverpool (L25 7SA)

As this neat, semi-detached, mock-Tudor suburban home testifies, and contrary to the 'Working Class Hero' media mythology, John Lennon, did _not_ come from 'the slums of Liverpool'.

The Second World War had just ended when John came to Mendips to be brought up by his Aunt Mimi and her dairy farmer husband, George. It was to be John's home until Beatle fame forced him to move to London in 1963. This was John's main home from the age of five until he was 23. He spent more time here than anywhere else in his 40-year life. Right until the end Mendips held a special place in John's heart.

It was here that he had been smitten by the rock and roll bug after hearing Elvis's _Heartbreak Hotel_ on Radio Luxembourg. If the charismatic, swivel-hipped Presley ignited the spark, it was the decidedly un-hip British skiffle singer Lonnie Donegan who fanned the flame.

The whole appeal of skiffle, based on three simple guitar chords, was that it was so easy, anybody could do it. John was no exception. From the time that he carefully unwrapped his first £10 'guaranteed not to split' mail order guitar, the die was cast. From then right up to his death in 1980 he was to be a rock and roll musician.

Soon John was writing songs of his own. _The One After 909_ was one early effort written whilst still at school. Other early songs written by John here in Mendips include _I Call Your Name_, _Hello Little Girl_ and _Please, Please Me_. John wrote this in his bedroom over the front porch. Just before his death he was to recall the exact day, even remembering the colour of the coverlet on his bed and Roy Orbison's _Only the Lonely_ which, along with Bing Crosby's _Please, lend your little ears to my pleas_ inspired him to write _Please, Please Me_, the first of an unbroken chain of twelve No.1 hits for the Beatles.

His authoritarian Aunt Mimi, pictured on page 71, did not encourage his new-found love affair with the guitar and regularly banished him and the peace-shattering instrument out of earshot to the glazed front porch with the admonition – "*The guitar's all very well John, but you'll never make a living out of it.*" Framed, Mimi's immortal words took pride of place in her bungalow overlooking Poole Harbour in Dorset. John bought her this luxury home in 1965 when the attentions of the growing army of fans laying siege to Mendips in the hope of a sighting of the famous Beatle became too much. She lived there until her death on 6 December 1991.

Today, all that remains are the memories. But just look at Mendips...and 'Imagine'. The carefree childhood days John spent here with Mimi, his doting uncle George, his three cats, Titch, Tim and Sam and the family mongrel dog Sally. The frequent visits from his 'real' mother, Julia, vivacious, carefree and a kindred free spirit. Imagine John, the rebellious teenager cycling to Quarry Bank School followed by tormented art student days as the archetypal 'angry young man'. And, later, John the family man living here with his wife Cynthia and new son Julian.

Opposite page – above left: the Lennon look early 1960s: black leather jacket and T-shirt, jeans and Rickenbacker guitar; right: Andy Wharhol artwork featured on the front cover of John's Menlove Avenue album released posthumously in 1986 under Yoko Ono's supervision; bottom: the lounge at Mendips restored by the National Trust to appear as it would have done when John was living here.

This page – left: the glazed porch used by John, and sometimes Paul, for practice sessions; centre: John stands in the porch at Mendips; right: recreation of John's bedroom, directly above the porch. Among the songs written here by John, and occasionally Paul, were 'Please Please Me', 'Good Day Sunshine', 'Hello Little Girl', and 'I Call Your Name'.

Imagine too, Paul, George and Pete Best knocking on the front door to join John in early Beatles rehearsals – with Mimi well out of the way, of course. And visits from their new manager, Brian Epstein. Imagine also the times John returned to Mendips drained from long nights in the seedy clubs of Hamburg, sweat-sodden from the cellar clubs of Liverpool and light-headed from tours carried along on waves of Beatlemania. Imagine it all.

And best of all, imagine, just imagine as, guitar in hand, Lennon the uncompromising genius sat on the edge of his bed (see above right) or stood in this porch (above left) creating and singing some of those classic songs for which the Beatles will forever be remembered.

On 9 December 2000, the 20th anniversary of John's death, an English Heritage blue plaque was unveiled by John's cousin and half-sisters. Even more important, Mendips was 'saved for the nation' when Yoko Ono bought it in 2002 following the death of the owner and immediately donated it to The National Trust. Built in 1933, many of Mendips' art-nouveau features have been retained and the National Trust has made a fine job of restoring the house to what it would have looked like when John lived here. Mendips has been open to visitors since March 2003. The National Trust organises a combined visit by mini-bus to Mendips and Paul's house at 20 Forthlin Road which start and finish in Liverpool city centre. This is a unique and truly wonderful experience and should not be missed. You should book in advance.

Booking arrangements: *On-line bookings – www.nationaltrust.org.uk/beatles Telephone bookings line – 0151 427 7231. Infoline – +44 (0)844 800 4791*

MENLOVE AVENUE — DEATH OF A DEAR MOTHER (L25 6EW)

It was dusk on that fine summer's evening – Tuesday 15 July 1958 – as John's mother Julia stood chatting to her sister Mimi at the gate of Mendips. At about 10pm they waved their goodbyes. Mimi went into the house and Julia headed towards the bus stop near The Vineries on the opposite side of the dual carriageway.

As she stepped from the grassed central reservation into the second carriageway of Menlove Avenue, her poor eyesight meant that she did not see the grey Standard Vanguard saloon car, registration number LKF 630, driven by off-duty Police Constable 126 Eric Clague, bearing down on her in the half-light.

Seconds later John's school friend Nigel Walley was at Mimi's door to deliver the grim news that her sister had been involved in an accident. Mimi dashed across to where Julia lay unconscious, her head in a pool of blood. Near the bus stop, a distance of 58 feet further back up the road, her bag and its contents poignantly marked the spot where she had been sent spinning through the air. Quickly, Mimi returned to Mendips for her coat and climbed into the ambulance that sped them through the Penny Lane roundabout and on to Sefton General Hospital.

Julia was pronounced 'dead on arrival'. The autopsy report noted a large fracture at the base of her skull which had exposed her brain, and there were other impact injuries.

Accounts of the tragedy were wildly contradictory. Constable Clague claimed that he had been travelling at well under 30 miles per hour, that Julia had walked into his path, that he had sounded his horn and had braked, that he had even mounted the central reservation, missing trees in the process, in a desperate bid to avoid hitting her. Two eye witnesses, a 15-year old shipping clerk and a man riding his bicycle in the same direction, told a completely different story. They both said the car was going very fast, that it did not sound its horn and that the brake lights did not come on.

Nigel Walley, the Quarrymen's occasional tea chest base player and their first manager, claimed that he had heard the screeching of brakes and a thud and had seen Julia flying through the air and landing about 100ft along the road (almost twice the distance given by the police to the Coroner).

The inquest, exactly one month after the accident, recorded a verdict of 'misadventure'. Constable Clague, a learner-driver who should have been accompanied by a qualified driver, later stood trial. He was acquitted but was suspended from the police service for a time.

For John, the 17-year old art student who had 're-discovered' the mother he had 'lost' as a child, this second loss – for good this time – was almost more than he could bear. Externally, it was expressed in heavy drinking and the aggressive and often cruel 'hard man' front that he presented to the world. Internally, his sensitive feelings were later to find an outlet in songs such as *Julia* and the heart-rending *Mother* – "You had me but I never had you."

The bus stop at the junction of Menlove Avenue and The Vineries where Julia had been heading for on that fateful evening.

ST. PETER'S CHURCH & HALL — JOHN MEETS PAUL FOR THE FIRST TIME: 'WHERE IT ALL BEGAN'. ELEANOR RIGBY'S GRAVE

Church Road, Woolton, Liverpool *(L25 6DA)*

This is the unlikely setting for the historic first meeting of the 20th century's two most famous singer/songwriters. On Saturday, 6 July 1957, the 15-year old Paul McCartney, wearing his flash white sport coat and black drainpipe trousers, cycled from his home in Allerton to St. Peter's church fete. He'd come at the suggestion of Ivan Vaughan, a class-mate, to see the Quarrymen, a skiffle group for which Ivan sometimes played tea chest bass. And, there might also be the chance of chatting up some girls.

That afternoon, in a field behind the church, John Lennon and his Quarrymen Skiffle Group sang their way through skiffle standards like *Railroad Bill*, *Cumberland Gap* and *Maggie May*, as well as rockers such as *Be Bop A Lula* and hits of the day like the Dell Vikings' *Come Go With Me*. Paul was mightily impressed even though John had stumbled over the words of every song and had to improvise.

Afterwards, in the church hall across the road (see p78) where the Quarrymen had been booked to play an evening gig, he was introduced to the group by Ivan Vaughan, a schoolmate of Paul and boyhood friend of John. Paul showed them how he played *Twenty Flight Rock*, *Be Bop a Lula* and other songs from his repertoire. Not only did Paul know all the words but he could play proper chords *and* tune a guitar, skills that had thus far eluded John Lennon.

Paul later recalled their first meeting..."I remember this beery old man getting nearer and breathing down me neck as I was playing. 'What's this old drunk doing?' I thought. Then he said *Twenty Flight Rock* was one of his favourites. So I knew he was a connoisseur. It was John. He'd just had a few beers. He was 16 and I was only 14 (just 15 actually), so he was a big man". "I remember him in a checked shirt with slightly curly hair and I thought: He looks good — I wouldn't mind being in a group with him." Years later, John was to say "That was the day, the day I met Paul that it started moving." That meeting was arguably the most important meeting in the history of popular music.

Although John had more or less decided that day that he wanted him in the Quarrymen, it was a week or so before the message was finally passed to Paul — "D'ya wanna join me group?" And it wasn't until 18 October that Paul eventually made his debut with the Quarrymen.

In the burial ground adjoining the church you will find the grave of Eleanor Rigby. Although Paul has given other sources for the origin of this name when writing his *Eleanor Rigby* No.1 hit, he has conceded that he may well have seen the Eleanor Rigby headstone during his frequent visits to St. Peter's churchyard to hang out with John so perhaps he was subconsciously influenced by it after all? The same would apply, even more so, to John who went to Sunday School here, sang in the church choir, was a member of its youth club and the Boy Scouts and had even been 'confirmed' here, pledging '...to live a life of committed discipleship'.

John's adored uncle, George Toogood Smith, Mimi's husband, who had been his stand-in father from the age of five until fourteen and who had bought him his first mouth organ, is also buried here; he had collapsed at Mendips and died soon after in hospital. He was only 52. Coincidentally, another *four* gravestones close to Eleanor Rigby's also carry the name 'Rigby' — it was quite a common name around Woolton. And, to add to the list of coincidences, a nearby gravestone bears another name from the *Eleanor Rigby* song: (Father) 'McKenzie'.

Just imagine...

16-year old John Lennon is fronting his skiffle group, the Quarrymen. In the audience is 15-year old Paul McCartney. It is the first time in his life he has clapped eyes on John but it was a moment he would never forget –

"I remember when we first met, at Woolton, at the village fete. It was a beautiful summer day and I walked in there and saw you on stage. And you were singing 'Come Go With Me' by the Del Vikings. But you didn't know the words so you made them up..." Paul

John: *"That was the day, the day I met Paul that it started moving."*

The time: Saturday, 6 July, 1957

The place: The field at the rear of St. Peter's Church, Woolton.

The occasion: The church's Summer fete and the historic first meeting of Lennon and McCartney, the 20th century's two most famous singer/songwriters.

Above left: St. Peter's Church Hall where Paul first met John; above right: a plaque on the wall of the church hall commemorates the occasion; below: the gravestone of Eleanor Rigby in the churchyard. Did Paul see it and did it subconsciously influence his choice of name for his 1966 classic No.1 hit 'Eleanor Rigby'?

As for the 'real' Eleanor Rigby, interred in this churchyard, she was born in 1895 and lived most of her life at 8 Vale Road, a few minutes' walk from Mendips – so how's that for a coincidence? Although she had lost her father around the time of her birth, she was not really the lonely woman in the song whose funeral nobody attended. In fact, her mother remarried and produced two stepsisters for her. She eventually married herself at the age of 35. She had no children of her own and was cut down in her prime in 1939 with a brain haemorrhage.

On the 40th anniversary of John and Paul's first encounter a weekend of special celebrations was held here. There was a garden fete, a memorabilia sale, John's original band, the Quarrymen, reformed and played a gig and a commemorative plaque was unveiled at the end of a special church service at St Peter's. The Queen, Prime Minister and Yoko, Cynthia and Paul were amongst the many who sent personal messages. The church hall's stage, where John and Paul played, is now on display in the Museum of Liverpool.

174 MACKETS LANE — GEORGE HARRISON'S HOUSE

Hunts Cross, Liverpool (L25 8TQ)

The Harrison family lived here between 1962 and 1965 during which time George and the Beatles soared to worldwide fame.

Like the other Beatle houses in the 60s this Council house became the focal point for George's fans. Fan mail by the sackload was delivered here and often the fans themselves turned up on the doorstep in the hope of a 'sighting'. Finally, in 1965, George's father quit his bus driver's job and the Harrisons moved into a house bought for them by George near Warrington.

1 BLOMFIELD ROAD — JULIA LENNON'S HOUSE

Liverpool (L19 4UY)

Unbeknown to John for a number of years, this is the house where his real mother Julia lived. It is less than two miles away from where he lived with her sister, his Aunt Mimi, who to all intents and purposes had been his mother since he was five.

The 1940s had been a turbulent period for Julia. It was wartime. She'd had a baby, John, been deserted by her sailor husband Freddie, 'given' John away to her sister to be brought up and had another wartime baby by a soldier. This child, Victoria Lennon, was born in the Salvation Army's 'Elmswood' Nursing Home, North Mossley Hill Road, Liverpool, in June 1945 and had immediately been adopted by a local woman and her husband, a Norwegian seaman. She was brought up as 'Ingrid Pedersen', in Crosby, North Liverpool. She never met her 'real' mother or father or famous half-brother John Lennon, although she met briefly with her two half-sisters in 2000 outside Mendips.

After the war Julia had formed a steady relationship with John 'Bobby' Dykins and had two daughters, Julia and Jacqueline, by him. It was a relationship that was to last for the rest of her life, even though it was never formalised by marriage: Julia never got round to divorcing the feckless Freddie Lennon.

During John's teenage years 1 Blomfield Road virtually became his second home. These were the years when he 're-discovered' his mother, although she was more like an older sister or fellow conspirator than a real mother. She was naturally musical and could play the piano, banjo, ukulele and accordion; for good measure, she could even juggle! Like John, she was a big Presley fan and even had a stray cat called Elvis.

Here, Julia taught John chords on the £11 cheap 'guaranteed not to split' Gallotone guitar she had bought him and which John can be seen playing at St. Peter's church fete (see page 76); it had not escaped Paul's notice that, not only was he mangling the words to the songs, but he was using banjo chords. Indeed, half-sister Julia recalled their mother teaching him Buddy Holly's *That'll Be The Day* on the banjo. Best of all, she never objected to John and his Quarrymen using her home to practice. The bathroom, where the sound of guitar and washboard would bounce off the hard tiles, was a favourite bolthole for the young musicians.

John frequently stayed here, sometimes for days at a time. During one occasion, on the night of 15 July 1958, a policeman knocked on the door to tell him and Bobby that Julia had been involved in a traffic accident. They rushed in a taxi to Sefton General Hospital, Smithdown Road, only to be told the horrible truth – the happy-go-lucky Julia was already dead. For the devastated 17-year old John, this was the second time in his young life that he'd 'lost' his mother, this time for good.

ALLERTON CEMETERY — JULIA LENNON'S GRAVE

Woolton Road, Liverpool (L19 5NF)

This is the final resting place of John's adored mother, Julia Lennon. She was buried here in Church of England Section 38, grave No.805, at 10am on Monday, 21 July 1958. She was 44 years of age, a woman in the prime of her life. The grave carries a simple stone marker inscribed 'Mummy' followed by the names of her four children: John, Victoria, Julia and Jackie. Julia is the only member of the family buried there. It is not known if John attended the funeral but he was at The Cottage, 120a Allerton Road, Woolton Village for post-funeral refreshments.

Almost nine, John is clearly delighted at the prospect of having his photograph taken with him his beloved mother Julia in the summer of 1949. At the time Julia is pregnant with her fourth child, Jackie.

Above: the National Trust has done a wonderful job of restoring 20 Forthlin Road to look like it did when it was the McCartney family home between 1956 and 1964. This is the lounge or, as we call it in Liverpool, the 'front room' or 'front parlour'; opposite page, Paul's bedroom: a favourite place for Paul and John to work on their new songs. Here he would sleep, dream of future fame as a rock and roll performer, study, practice guitar and hone his song-writing skills.

The McCartney family had moved house many times over the years but it was definitely a step up in the world when, at the end of April 1956, they moved from the tough Speke housing estate to Forthlin Road off Mather Avenue in the genteel leafy suburb of Allerton (rent £1.19.10d per week).

Mrs McCartney was delighted with her new home and was over the moon that Mike as well as Paul had won places to the Liverpool Institute, reputedly the best grammar school in the city. Her joy was to be very short-lived. Along came 'Maxwell with his silver hammer' and she died of breast cancer after a short illness on 31 October 1956, leaving bereft husband Jim to bring up 14-year old Paul and his younger brother Mike. Mary's grave can be found in Yew Tree Cemetery, Section 3A, Grave 276. Tragically, Paul's wife Linda was also to fall victim to breast cancer in 1998. With Paul's backing, the Linda McCartney Centre, which provides specialist treatment for breast and others cancers, was opened two years later at the Royal Liverpool University Hospital.

In this house Paul was to 'lose' himself in his guitar, even taking it to the bathroom where the excellent acoustics compensated for the lack of an amplifier. After Paul's historic first encounter with John Lennon at St. Peter's church garden fete, Woolton, on 6 July 1957, this house became a favourite rehearsal venue for the newly-formed, but soon to be formidable, Lennon and McCartney song-writing partnership. They wrote some twenty songs here, including *I Saw Her Standing There*, before their first single *Love Me Do* gave them chart success.

Unlike John's Aunt Mimi, Paul's dad was himself no mean musician and actively encouraged the boys. In any case he was at work all day at A. Hannay & Co., cotton brokers with offices at 14 Chapel Street, just around the corner from the Liverpool Cotton Exchange. And when the cat's away... and play they certainly did. Here, in the front room of this house, Paul and John, sitting opposite each other with acoustic guitars in hand, would collaborate on the dozens of songs to be written down in school exercise books: 'Another Lennon / McCartney original'. At other times they would draw each other, raid the larder, bring girls back and even smoke Typhoo tea in Jim's pipe.

After the Beatles returned from their triumphant American tour in 1964, Paul bought his dad 'Rembrandt', a very 'des res' in Baskervyle Road in posh Heswall on the Wirral. With a removal van ordered for midnight, the Macs avoided the attentions of fans, media and curious neighbours by doing a moonlight flit.

Because of its importance in the history of popular music, The National Trust bought this house when it came on the market in 1996. This was a controversial 'first' for the Trust which is noted for rescuing great historic houses and grand country estates rather than humble suburban council houses. Much altered over the years, the house has been restored to what it looked like when the McCartneys lived here. Visitors are treated to an exhibition of Mike's nostalgic photographs of family life at Forthlin Road, an audio tour and a display of Beatles memorabilia. A visit is highly recommended. For details of The National Trust's bus tours, which include joint entry to 20 Forthlin Road and Mendips, see page 73.

FORMER WILSON HALL — GEORGE'S FIRST MEETING WITH JOHN AND THE QUARRYMEN

Speke Road, Garston, Liverpool (L19 2PA)

Re-built as a Lennon's supermarket (no relation), and for many years the Woolton Carpet Centre, this was the site of Wilson Hall where the Quarrymen played four times to a largely local audience of Teddy boy roughnecks.

More significantly, it was here, on 6 February 1958, that an embryonic 14-year old teddy boy by the name of George Harrison first saw the Quarrymen and was introduced by Paul to their leader John Lennon, impressing him with his rendition of Bill Justis' instrumental hit *Raunchy* with its memorable guitar riff. However, Paul's version of George's 'audition' has it that he, John and George were travelling on the top deck of a Liverpool Corporation bus when, spurred on by Paul, George took out his guitar and played *Raunchy* sufficiently well for John to offer him the job of 'lead guitarist' with the Quarrymen.

SPEKE AREA

LIVERPOOL JOHN LENNON AIRPORT Speke, Liverpool (L24 1YD)

This was the Beatles' local airport. However, the terminal building they used in those days, some distance away in Speke Road, opposite the retail park, is now an hotel.

In 1962 the Beatles flew from here to London to record *Love Me Do*, their first chart success. But the highlight for the airport came on 10 July 1964 when the Beatles flew in to a 'proper' airport reception of the kind previously witnessed at London's Heathrow and New York's John F Kennedy airports, complete with screaming fans and a press reception.

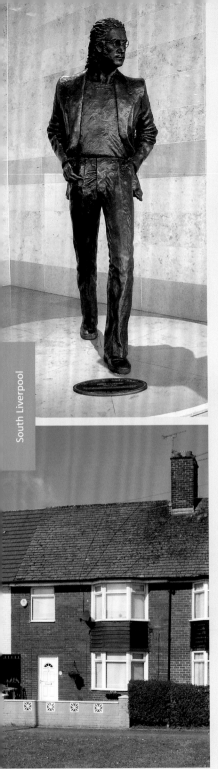

Left: Tom Murphy's interpretation of John Lennon.
Bottom: 72 Western Avenue, Speke.

Liverpool Airport became the first in the UK to be named after an individual when, in July 2001, Yoko Ono visited the airport to announce its renaming as 'Liverpool John Lennon Airport'. Ringo later quipped that he'd like to have one of the baggage handling conveyor belts named after him!

In March 2002 Yoko returned to the Airport to unveil a 7ft bronze statue of John by local sculptor Tom Murphy. The imposing statue is sited on the main passenger walkway overlooking the check-in hall.

Outside the airport's terminal building is another reminder to visitors that Liverpool is 'Beatle City', a giant replica of the Yellow Submarine.

72 WESTERN AVENUE — PAUL'S HOUSE *Speke, Liverpool (L24 3US)*

Paul's mother, Mary, had been allocated this terraced house, rent-free as a perk of working locally as a midwife on the giant new Speke housing estate. The McCartneys moved here from their flat in Sir Thomas White Gardens, Everton, in August 1947 when Paul was five. Among the tricks he and brother Mike got up to was to throw stones at their neighbour's tree 'to speed up the growth of the apples'! The McCartneys lived here until late 1950 when Mary packed in her job as a midwife and became Speke's Health Visitor. She was allocated another Council house at Speke, 12 Ardwick Road.

STOCKTON WOOD PRIMARY SCHOOL — PAUL'S FIRST SCHOOL

All Saints Road, Speke, Liverpool (L24 3TF)

A short walk from Paul's home in Western Avenue, this was his first school. The post-war 'baby boom' pushed the school population over the 1,500 saturation level making it the biggest infants school in England, at which stage, in September 1951, Paul and his brother Mike were moved to the Joseph Williams Primary School in Gateacre. The original school buildings have been replaced by a modern primary school.

12 ARDWICK ROAD — PAUL'S HOUSE *Speke, Liverpool (L24 2UA)*

After Western Avenue, the McCartneys moved to this new Council house in Autumn 1950 before finally leaving the sprawling Speke estate for Forthlin Road in 1955. Living just around the corner from here in Upton Green was George who often travelled on the same bus as Paul to their school, the Liverpool Institute. George recalled – "So Paul and I used to be on the same bus, in the same school uniform, travelling home from the Liverpool Institute. I discovered that he had a trumpet and he found out that I had a guitar, and we got together. I was about thirteen."

25 UPTON GREEN — GEORGE'S HOUSE *Speke, Liverpool (L24 2UL)*

The Harrison family had been on Liverpool Corporation's housing waiting list for 18 years when, the day after New Year's Day 1950, they at last moved to this new house. Compared with their tiny 'two up, two down' house in a back street cul-de-sac in Wavertree, this house seemed palatial to George. And there was a 'green' where children could play safely under the watchful eyes of their mothers.

George was six years old at the time and this was to be his home until 1 October 1962 when the family moved to Mackets Lane in Hunts Cross, near Woolton. Luckily, George's mother positively approved of his struggle to master the guitar so this was always a favourite house for practice sessions.

At the nearby British Legion Club in Damwood Road in 1957, the Rebels, comprising George, his brother Peter and two friends, played skiffle numbers for their one and only gig there for the princely sum of ten shillings (fifty pence) each.

George first heard the broadcasting of the Beatles' first hit record *Love Me Do*, released in October 1962, in this house, running upstairs with the radio and yelling to his mum and dad, "It's on! It's on!". It was a landmark in his life, as he later recalled – "First hearing *Love Me Do* on the radio sent me shivery all over. It was the best buzz of all time."

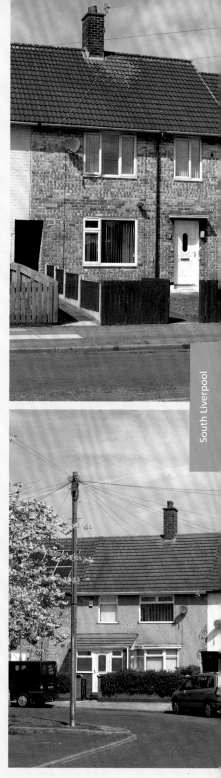

South Liverpool

North and East Liverpool

NORTH AND EAST LIVERPOOL

1. The Collegiate
2. Grafton & Locarno
3. Percy Phillips' Recording Studio
4. Beatle Streets
5. 10 Sunbury Road
6. Walton Hospital
7. Jewish Cemetery
8. Casbah Club
9. Broadway Con' Club
10. Lathom Hall
11. Litherland Town Hall
12. Huyton Parish Church Cemetery

SEAFORTH

LITHERLAND

BOOTLE

ORRELL PARK

AINTREE

FAZAKERLEY

WALTON

ANFIELD

NORRIS GREEN

WEST DERBY VILLAGE

KNOTTY ASH

HUYTON VILLAGE

EVERTON

CITY CENTRE

RIVER MERSEY

CROSBY ROAD NORTH
PRINCESS WAY
HAWTHORNE ROAD
KNOWSLEY ROAD
NORTHFIELD ROAD
MOSS LANE
MERTON ROAD
DERBY ROAD
BREEZE HILL
WALTON ROAD
COUNTY ROAD
RICE LANE
LONG LANE
WALTON VALE
STOPGATE LANE
PARTHENON DRIVE
STRAWBERRY ROAD
QUEENS DRIVE
LORENZO DRIVE
BROAD LANE
ALMONDS GREEN
TOWN ROW
QUEENS DRIVE
BLACKMOOR DRIVE
EAST PRESCOT ROAD
LIVERPOOL ROAD
BLUE BELL LANE
LONGVIEW LANE
HUYTON LANE
KIRKDALE ROAD
HEYWORTH STREET
SCOTLAND ROAD
LEEDS STREET
ISLINGTON
LONDON ROAD
PRESCOT STREET
KENSINGTON
EVERTON ROAD
BRECK ROAD
WALTON BRECK ROAD
TOWNSEND LANE
WEST DERBY ROAD
MURHEAD AVENUE
GREAT HOWARD STREET

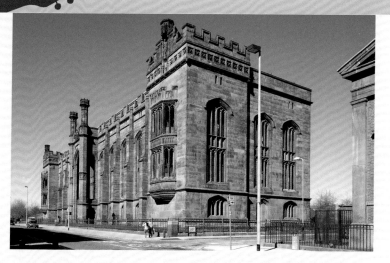

FORMER COLLEGIATE — PETE BEST'S GRAMMAR SCHOOL

Shaw Street, Liverpool (L6 1HA)

The Collegiate, opened in 1843, vied with the Liverpool Institute for the reputation of being the best grammar school in the city. Pete Best, who had been born in India and came to Liverpool at the age of four, was a pupil here from age eleven until he was a sixth form student, leaving in 1958. The following year he met the frequently drummerless Quarrymen – John, Paul and George – and the year after that he finally joined the Beatles for their first trip to Hamburg. The Collegiate has been redeveloped into private apartments for inner city living; happily the imposing original facade of the building has been retained.

THE GRAFTON AND LOCARNO BALLROOMS

West Derby Road, Liverpool (L6 9BY)

The 'Loc' (now re-named the Liverpool Olympia), and next door neighbour, the 'Gravvie' – once known for its 'Grab-a-granny' nights – were two of a number of large, popular 'palais de dance' venues on the fringe of the city centre where the Quarrymen and later the Beatles played during the late 50s and early 60s .

When the Beatles first performed at the 'Loc' on 14 February 1963 at a special St. Valentine's Night dance, they had already recorded their *Please, Please Me* album. They appeared four times at the 'Gravvie', first on 3 August 1962 with their parting gig taking place a year later on 2 August 1963. This was to be their final Merseyside dance hall date. The following night would see their last-ever appearance at the Cavern. By then their fourth single *She Loves You* was being prepared for release the following month. It was to be a mega hit on both sides of the Atlantic.

'BEATLE STREETS' *Kensington Fields Estate, Liverpool (L6 9HT)*

Four streets on this 1981 private housing estate have been named after the Beatles: John Lennon Drive, Paul McCartney Way, George Harrison Close and Ringo Starr Close. There's also an Epstein Court and, coincidentally, nearby you will find Sutcliffe Street although it has no association with Stu Sutcliffe.

PERCY PHILLIPS' RECORDING STUDIO *38 Kensington, Liverpool (L7 8XB)*

Although definitely not in the same league as his namesake Sam Phillips' Sun Studio in Memphis, where Elvis Presley recorded some 24 songs, nevertheless this is where John, Paul and George and two other Quarrymen made their very first record in July 1958, a cover of Buddy Holly's *That'll Be The Day* and a McCartney/Harrison original *In Spite Of All The Danger*. John sang the lead on both sides. Just one acetate copy was made and it is now owned by Paul. John, Paul and George were back here again in 1960 to cut a Lennon original, *The One After 909*. Sadly, that recording seems to have been lost.

10 SUNBURY ROAD – PAUL'S FIRST HOUSE *Anfield, Liverpool (L4 2TT)*

Jim and Mary McCartney moved into furnished rooms here after their wartime wedding in April 1941. It was to this house in June of the following year that the newly-born Paul was brought from Walton Hospital.

FORMER WALTON HOSPITAL – PAUL'S BIRTHPLACE

Clocktower Drive, off Rice Lane, Liverpool (general hospital services now part of Aintree Hospitals) (L9 1EP)

Birthplace of Beatle Paul or, to give him his full name, James Paul McCartney. Paul's mother, Mary, had once been a sister on the maternity ward here and had qualified for a private ward for the birth of Paul, her first child, on 18 June 1942. It was a difficult birth and, deprived of oxygen, baby Paul had to be resuscitated as an

emergency. Happily, he quickly recovered and, as he is now in his 70s, it is clear he suffered no lasting damage. Both of Paul's parents were in their thirties when they married – Jim was 39, Mary 32. Paul's brother Peter, but known for most of his life as Mike, was also born here, on 7 January 1944.

Paul's birth certificate was sold at a Bonham's auction in Tokyo in March 1997 for a staggering £51,715. Paul was understandably miffed to put it mildly that, quite literally, his birthright had been 'stolen' from under him.

In the 1990s, Walton Hospital merged with Fazackerley Hospital and its general medical services were relocated there two miles away in what is now known as Aintree University Hospitals. All that remains of Walton Hospital, originally a workhouse, is the 1860s landmark clock tower building, now converted into apartments.

Opposite page – Top: 38 Kensington; Centre: 10 Sunbury Road; Bottom: The landmark Clock Tower of the former Walton Hospital; Below: Brian Epstein's grave in the Long Lane Jewish Cemetery.

JEWISH CEMETERY – BRIAN EPSTEIN'S GRAVE

Long Lane, Aintree, Liverpool *(L9 7DT)*
(opposite Taskers/adjacent to Everton Cemetery*)*

Following his tragic death at his London flat from an overdose of the drug Carbrital on 27 August 1967 at the age of 32, Brian Epstein's body was carried from Liverpool's Greenbank Drive Synagogue and buried here in Grave H12, Section A.

Along with the Epstein family at the graveside ceremony at 7pm on 29 August were a number of Brian's favourites – Cilla Black, Gerry (of Gerry and the Pacemakers) and Nat Weiss, his American friend and lawyer. In defiance of the Jewish rule forbidding flowers at funerals, Weiss tossed a newspaper containing a single hidden white chrysanthemum onto Brian's coffin, a farewell request from George on behalf of the Beatles.

Brian's father, mother and brother are also buried here.

8 HAYMAN'S GREEN — PETE BEST'S HOUSE & CASBAH COFFEE CLUB

West Derby, Liverpool (L12 7JG)

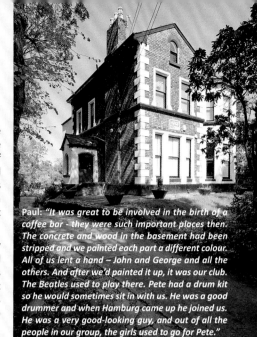

On 29 August 1959, as the Quarrymen, John, Paul and George performed at the opening night of this social club for teenagers created in the basement of Mona 'Mo' Best's rambling Victorian house. From then until June 1962 they played 44 gigs at the Casbah.

Mo's son had also been smitten by the rock and roll bug and played drums with his Blackjacks group. His name was Pete Best and by August 1960 he had joined the Beatles as their new drummer on their first trip to Hamburg.

Paul: *"It was great to be involved in the birth of a coffee bar - they were such important places then. The concrete and wood in the basement had been stripped and we painted each part a different colour. All of us lent a hand – John and George and all the others. And after we'd painted it up, it was our club. The Beatles used to play there. Pete had a drum kit so he would sometimes sit in with us. He was a good drummer and when Hamburg came up he joined us. He was a very good-looking guy, and out of all the people in our group, the girls used to go for Pete."*

Two years later, on 16 August 1962, to the fury of his many fans, he was unceremoniously dumped by the Beatles in favour of Ringo Starr. Too good looking and popular with girl fans? Not up to the mark as a drummer? Didn't fit in with the personalities of John, Paul and George, a close-knit trio since the Quarrymen days? To this day Pete Best is adamant that he still doesn't know exactly why he was sacked. Suffice it to say that none of the Beatles were prepared to tell Pete to his face; they left the dirty work to Brian Epstein. Less than a month later they had recorded *Love Me Do* and were on their way to fame and fortune leaving behind a devastated Pete. Happily, he did not allow this crushing blow to embitter him for long. Earlier that same year, on 24 January 1962, Pete, along with John, Paul and George, had gathered here with Brian Epstein for the formal signing of the Beatles' original management contract. For Pete, his dream of stardom was over.

Certainly to his girl fans, Pete, with his dark, moody film star looks – he reminded me of a young, but black-haired, Jeff Chandler – was far and away 'The Best of the Beatles'. It was not unknown for love-struck teenage girls to sleep in the front garden here simply to be near him.

Unlike John, Paul, George and Ringo, Randolph Peter Best, to give him his full name, was born, not in Liverpool, but in Madras, India, on 24 November 1941. The family came to Liverpool at Christmas 1945, living first in a flat above Egerton's pub in Cases Street (demolished), then to houses in West Derby at Princess Drive and 17 Queenscourt Road, where they lived for eight years before finally settling at 8 Hayman's Green in the ancient village of West Derby in 1957.

Pete, a family man and retired Civil Servant, has made quite a few appearances as a guest speaker at Beatle conventions over the years, including one I organised in 1985. More interestingly, he formed his Pete Best Band and has toured worldwide. Royalties from *The Beatles Anthology*, where Pete's drumming is featured on ten tracks, has meant that, over 30 years on, Pete was finally able to reap considerable financial reward from recordings made during his days with the early Beatles.

Left: Pete Best pictured at the Tower Ballroom, New Brighton, 21 June 1962.

North & East Liverpool

THE TRUE BEGINNINGS

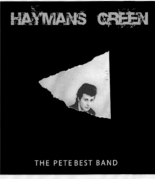
HAYMANS GREEN
THE PETE BEST BAND

In 2002, Pete and brothers, Roag and Rory, produced their excellent book 'The Beatles The True Beginnings'. The cover (above) shows the Quarrymen (drummerless) performing at the Casbah's opening night – L to R: George, Paul, Ken Brown and John.

The Pete Best Band's 'Haymans Green' album was also released in 2002 to mostly favourable reviews. Fittingly, the final track on the album is also called 'Hayman's Green'.

By all accounts, Pete's mother, Mo, was a formidable character with a strong 'can do' personality. She was not averse to taking risks either. In 1954 she pawned her jewellery and put the proceeds on a horse in one of the most famous races in the world, the Derby. The horse was *Never Say Die* and its jockey was 18-year old Lester Piggott. An outsider, the horse nevertheless flew past the winning post with odds of 33-1. Mo used her winnings to buy 8 Hayman's Green in 1957.

To mark the 40th anniversary of the Casbah Coffee Club in 1999, local Merseybeat-era bands performed for fans in the grounds of this house. They were also able to see ceiling and wall paintings by the Beatles and Cynthia Lennon. A replica of part of the Casbah was also installed in the Beatles Story museum at Albert Dock. Due to its historic Beatles connections, 8 Hayman's Green was given Grade Two Listed building status in 2006.

Today, some six decades later, the Casbah is still owned by the Best family and is open to visitors for pre-booked guided tours. For further information and details of visiting arrangements, visit Pete's website *www.petebest.com*

CLUBMOOR CONSERVATIVE MEN'S CLUB – PAUL'S FIRST GIG WITH JOHN AND THE QUARRYMEN

Back Broadway, Utting Avenue East, Liverpool (L11 1DQ)

Previously, as the New Clubmoor Hall, this saw 15-year old Paul's very first appearance with John and the Quarrymen, on 18 October 1957. It was an occasion memorable because Paul, on his first instrumental solo, had a bad attack of nerves, got 'sticky fingers' and fluffed *Guitar Boogie*. The incident marked the end of his career as a solo guitarist. Paul: "It wiped me out as a lead guitar player that night".

LATHOM HALL *Lathom Avenue, Seaforth, Liverpool (L21 1EB)*

Once a cinema, this was yet another of the unprepossessing suburban 'jive halls' on the early Beatles circuit. It is notable for being the first officially advertised gig for the 'Silver Beats', on 21 May 1960. However, it was one they never played since they were in Scotland on the final leg of the Johnny Gentle tour.

As the Silver Beats, they had played an interval spot the week previously and went on to play a few more engagements early in 1961. That first night, base player Stu Sutcliffe had been roughed up in a fight. John and Pete Best had gone to his rescue and John ended up with a broken finger. There is an oft-repeated story that Stu had been kicked in the head and that this resulted in his death from a brain haemorrhage two years later in Hamburg. According to Pete Best who says that he witnessed the incident, this is a myth.

LITHERLAND TOWN HALL — BIRTHPLACE OF 'BEATLEMANIA'

Hatton Hill Road, Litherland, Liverpool (L21 9JN)

Litherland Town Hall (pictured below), completely altered during its revamp as an NHS Health Centre, hosted scores of Beatles gigs during 1961. However, one gig towards the end of 1960 can lay claim to this building being 'The Birthplace of Beatlemania'.

The historic occasion took place on 27 December 1960. In a £6 booking arranged by Bob Wooler and billed as 'Direct from Hamburg – the sensational BEATLES!', the leather-clad Beatles brought the house down from the very start with a blistering rendition of *Long Tall Sally*. The dance hall crowd rushed to the stage invoking early scenes of the 'Beatlemania' that went on to sweep through the country and encircle the globe. Fame and fortune were surely now on the horizon.

The Beatles had only played North Liverpool once before and many in the audience that night really did believe that they were a German group. Local promoter Brian Kelly knew when he was on to a good thing and immediately booked them for no less than 36 dances over the next three months. It was to establish them as Merseyside's top rock and roll band.

They played their final gig here on the evening of another historic day, 9 November 1961. As the Beatles were playing a lunchtime session at the Cavern that day, Brian Epstein came to see what all the fuss was about. As they say, the rest is history.

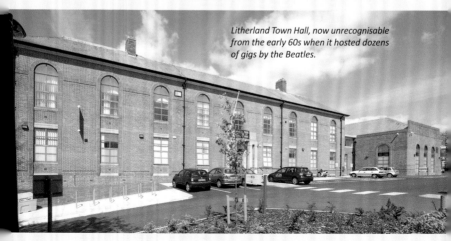

Litherland Town Hall, now unrecognisable from the early 60s when it hosted dozens of gigs by the Beatles.

North & East Liverpool

93

HUYTON PARISH CHURCH CEMETERY — STU SUTCLIFFE'S
GRAVE *Stanley Road/Blue Bell Lane, Huyton, Liverpool (L36 7SA)*

Although Stu Sutcliffe died in Hamburg on 10 April 1962, aged just 21 years and 10 months, he was not buried there. His final resting place is in this cemetery, grave number 552 in section 1939 where he was laid to rest on 19 April 1962. The other members of the Beatles missed the funeral as they were playing at the Star Club in Hamburg. Stu had been a member of the church youth club and its choir at this church until his voice broke.

The entrance to the graveyard is tucked away in the corner at the junction of Blue Bell Lane and Stanley Road, across the road from the church itself. As you enter the graveyard, there is a Stuart Sutcliffe memorial bench immediately to the right which was installed in 2015, 53 years after his death. Stuart's grave is about six rows from the back of the graveyard, a little to the left of centre. Stuart's father, Charles, died four years later in 1966 and is also buried here.

Visitors wanting to see the grave should phone 0151 449 3900 to check that the graveyard is open.

The inscription on the bench reads, "In loving memory of Stuart Sutcliffe 23.06.1940 – 10.04.1962 – 21 years old. Painter, poet, artist, musician and founder member of the Beatles. Love from family and fans.

Below: "Their name liveth for evermore". Prophetic. On 16 August 1960, en route from Liverpool to play their first gigs in Hamburg, the Beatles and their travelling companions stopped at the Allied war cemetery at Oosterbeek, Holland, to pay their respects to those who had fallen at the Battle of Arnhem. Pictured, left to right, are the Beatles' manager at that time, Allan Williams, his wife Beryl, Harold Phillips, better known as 'Lord Woodbine', Stu Sutcliffe, Paul McCartney, George Harrison and the Beatles' brand new drummer, Pete Best. John was there but opted to stay out of the photograph.

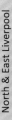

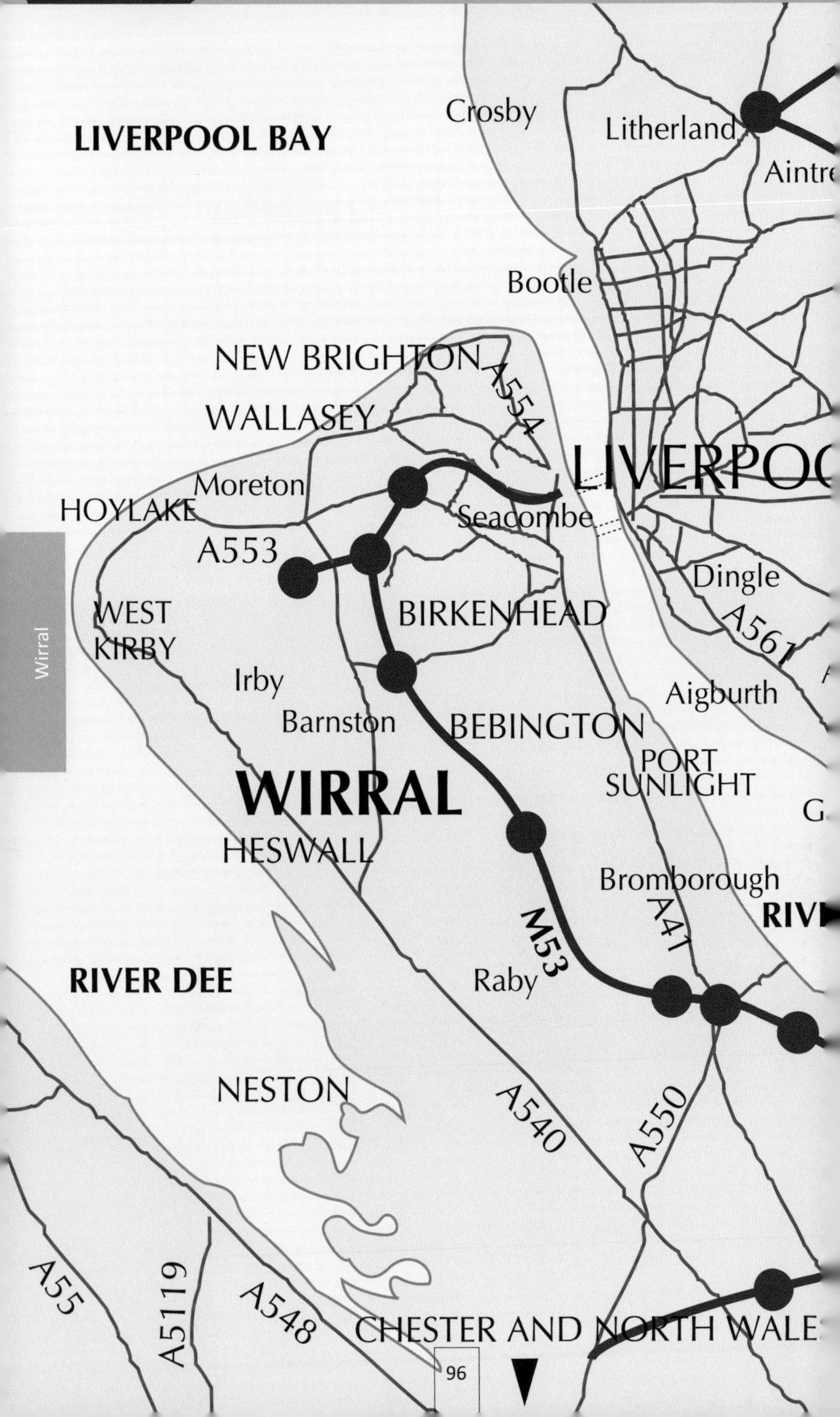

LIVERPOOL BAY

Crosby

Litherland

Aintre

NEW BRIGHTON

Bootle

A554

WALLASEY

Moreton

Seacombe

LIVERPOO

HOYLAKE

A553

Dingle

A561

BIRKENHEAD

WEST
KIRBY

Aigburth

Irby

Barnston

BEBINGTON

PORT
SUNLIGHT

WIRRAL

G

HESWALL

Bromborough

A41

RIV

RIVER DEE

M53

Raby

NESTON

A540

A550

A55

A5119

A548

CHESTER AND NORTH WALE

Wirral

BEATLE PLACES TO VISIT 'ACROSS THE WATER' IN WIRRAL

Wirral, the peninsula that lies between the River Mersey and the River Dee, is by far the most rurally, and coastally, scenic of Merseyside's five 'boroughs'. Although the Mersey may seem like a barrier, two road tunnels, an underground electric railway, a ferryboat service and even a road and rail bridge at Runcorn, mean that travelling between Liverpool and Wirral is a breeze.

When Merseysiders want a day out on their doorstep, they head for either Wirral or Southport. When they were young the Beatles were no exception; favourite playgrounds for them were the beaches of New Brighton and Wallasey.

Deceptively genteel, Wirral can lay claim to a number of Beatle 'firsts'. These include the very first time John, Paul, George and their new drummer, Ringo, performed on stage together, the first time they played in suits, the first booking organised for them by their new manager, Brian Epstein, their first ever radio interview and the first time they shared the bill with the rock and roll superstars of their day, such as Little Richard and Bruce Channel.

Hats off to Wirral Borough Council for fixing plaques to a number of sites of Beatle interest, including the Grosvenor Ballroom, Majestic Ballroom, Hulme Hall, Victoria Hall, Irby Village Hall, Macdona Hall, Apollo Roller Rink and the Tower Ballroom site.

FORMER MAJESTIC BALLROOM *Conway Street, Birkenhead (CH41 6JD)*

Now a Chinese restaurant, this was once a prestigious venue operated by the Top Rank organisation and an important one for the Beatles. They made seventeen appearances here between June 1962 and April 1963, perhaps the most memorable being on 15 December when they were crowned 1962's undisputed 'Kings of Mersey

Wirral

SENSATIONAL NEWS!!

THE BEATLES
(PARLOPHONE RECORDING GROUP)
...be playing a season of Thursday night engagements, starting
THURSDAY, 28th JUNE, 1962
at Merseyside's luxury ballroom
MAJESTIC, Conway Street, BIRKENHEAD
(only 10 minutes by train or boat from Liverpool)
...ANK DANCING   Manager: Bill Marsden

Beat' at the first *Mersey Beat* poll awards show. Runners up were Lee Curtis and the All Stars whose drummer was the recently deposed Pete Best. The photograph above shows Bill Harry, Editor of the Mersey Beat newspaper, presenting the Beatles with their trophy, the first of many the group would win in the years ahead.

FORMER BENO DORN'S TAILOR'S SHOP

17-19 Grange Road, Birkenhead (CH41 4BY)

On Monday afternoon the 29 January 1962, as part of his 'smarten up' strategy, Brian Epstein brought all four Beatles to be fitted out with snazzy new suits here at award-winning Beno Dorn's tailor's shop. Goodbye hot, sweaty and, no doubt, smelly leather. Hello well-cut, Italian-style dark blue mohair suits with narrow lapels and cuffs on the sleeves and 'drainpipe' trousers without turnups. And there were crisp white shirts, cuff links, collar pins and black knitted 'Sammy' ties to complete the 'cool dude' look. On Tuesday 6 March they were back here to pick up their new outfits; the following day they wore them for the very first time in front of a teenage audience during the live recording of the BBC's *Teenager's Turn – Here We Go* radio programme in Manchester.

GROSVENOR BALLROOM *Grosvenor Street, Wallasey (CH44 1AQ)*

Another suburban dance hall that finally yielded, at least temporarily, under the onslaught of rock 'n' roll by the likes of Gerry and the Pacemakers and the Beatles who played here 14 times during 1960 and 1961. Memorable because the gig on 10 March 1961 was the very last one booked for them by their then manager, Allan Williams a.k.a. 'The Man Who Gave Away the Beatles'.

THE GROSVENOR
This Plaque
Is To
Commemorate That
THE BEATLES
Played Regularly Here
Between
June 1960 & Sept 1961

It was also memorable for the punches which were often swung during its 'Swing Sessions'. Paul: "The Grosvenor Ballroom in Wallasey was one of the worst places; there would be a hundred Wallasey lads squaring up to a hundred lads from Seacombe and all hell would break loose. I remember one night a rumble had started before I

realised what was happening. I ran to the stage to save my Elpico amp, my pride and joy at the time. There were fists flying everywhere. One Ted grabbed me and said 'Don't move, or you're bloody dead!' I was scared for my life but I had to get that amp." In those days you could book the Beatles for about £10.

ALBERT MARRION'S FORMER PHOTOGRAPHIC STUDIO

268 Wallasey Village, Wallasey (CH45 3HB)

Dressed in their full black leathers and black T-shirts, the Beatles posed for publicity photographs in Albert Marrion's studio located above what is now a pizza shop on Sunday, 17 December 1961 – see below left. This, the Beatles' first professional studio photo shoot, was organised by Brian Epstein who was on hand to direct the session. Marrion also operated another studio...in Liverpool's Penny Lane.

FORMER PALAIS DE DANSE, APOLLO ROLLER RINK AND DANCE CLUB **195 Pasture Rd, Moreton, Wirral** (CH46 4TH)

This odd little building (bottom right) has been here for over a century and was the venue for just one Beatles gig on Monday 26 March 1962. Earlier that day the Beatles had played a lunchtime session at the Cavern. In those days, the Apollo was mainly a roller skating rink that had started to host rock 'n' roll nights on Mondays.

This Beatles childhood-era photograph, taken from New Brighton pier, shows the Tower Ballroom, funfair, promenade and beach on a busy summer's day. Below: plaque on the promenade in front of the site of the Tower Ballroom and poster for Operation Big Beat 5, 14 September 1962.

FORMER TOWER BALLROOM *Promenade, New Brighton (CH45 2PP)*

The Beatles played numerous gigs at this enormous ballroom between 1961 and 1963, most notably for local promoter Sam Leach's ambitious 'Operation Big Beat' shows which featured up to twelve acts on the one bill. The ballroom's sprung dance floor could easily accommodate 1,000 jiving couples.

The highlight of the Beatles' many appearances here was undoubtedly on 12 October 1962, the week after '*Love Me Do*' had been released, when they were second on the bill to one of their all-time heroes, Little Richard. Embarrassingly, the recently-ousted Pete Best was also there that night – as drummer with Lee Curtis and the All Stars. On other occasions the Beatles shared the stage with Bruce Channel, Joe Brown & his Bruvvers and, wait for it, the Clan McLeod Pipe Band!

A spectacular fire in 1969 marked the final end of the Tower Ballroom and Grounds. When it opened in 1900, the 567ft tower, modelled on the Eiffel Tower, was the tallest structure in the country. There was even a Parisian Tea Garden in the grounds. However, the tower had been operating for less than 20 years when the rot started to set in; literally, it was being eaten away by rust and the entire structure was dismantled.

THE BEATLES
Played at the
Tower Ballroom,
New Brighton
on 27 occasions

1961-1963

Victoria Hall.

18 TRINITY ROAD — CYNTHIA LENNON'S HOME

Hoylake *(CH47 2BT)*

Pictured above left, this was Cynthia Powell's modest family home where she was living when she and John Lennon met at the Liverpool College of Art and embarked on a passionate teenage love affair.

Once, following a vigorous love-making session in Stu Sutcliffe's flat, she ended up in the nearby Hoylake Cottage Hospital with grumbling appendicitis. She was visited by a concerned John, although for his first visit he brought George along too! Afterwards, John and George called here to tuck into plates of egg and chips served up by Cynthia's widowed mother — Cynthia's father died of lung cancer when she was 17. She was also a heavy smoker and died of cancer in 2015 at the age of 75.

Here Cynthia eagerly awaited the arrival of John's letters from Hamburg described by him as "The sexiest this side of Henry Miller. Forty pages long some of them".

After leaving Mendips this became 'home' for Cynthia (now Mrs Cynthia Lennon), Julian and John, although he was almost constantly on the road at this time. During this period John took Cynthia on a belated Parisian honeymoon. Soon after they returned, the Press discovered that they were married and laid siege to the house in the hope of a sighting of the famous Beatle with his new wife and baby Julian. With John away, Cynthia had Julian – full name John (after his father), Charles (after Cynthia's father) Julian Lennon – christened in December 1963 at nearby Holy Trinity Church (demolished). Although he wasn't at the christening, John and Cyn readily agreed to Brian Epstein's wish to become Julian's godfather. The following month John, Cyn and Julian moved to London.

VICTORIA HALL *Victoria Hall Walk, off Village Road, Bebington (CH63 8RH)*

The Beatles played this out-of-the-way venue just once, on Saturday 4 August 1962. This was to be one of Pete Best's last gigs as their drummer. A fortnight later they were back on the Wirral to play Hulme Hall in Port Sunlight Village. By then they had sacked Pete and new drummer Ringo Starr was about to make his debut.

Above top: The ante-room to the gentlemen's lavatory was the makeshift studio for this local hospital radio interview when the Beatles appeared at Hulme Hall on Saturday 27 October 1962. During the interview Paul confirms that John is indeed the leader of the group. Note the smart Beno Dorn suits and elastic-sided suede boots. This was to be the last of four Hulme Hall gigs.

Above: After the interview the Beatles went on stage to perform before their clearly adoring, and mostly female, fans. John and George confer, no doubt about what their next song would be: perhaps their newly-released first single 'Love Me Do'? These two photographs were the only ones taken that night by Liverpool photographer Don Valentine – in those days some professionals still carried bulky plate cameras and fragile glass slides, which tended to be used sparingly.

The following night, Sunday 28 October, the stakes were much higher. For the first time as the Beatles they were to play the Liverpool Empire alongside big stars such as Little Richard, one of their heroes. They had finally hit the big time, certainly in the city of their birth.

HULME HALL — 'BIRTH OF THE BEATLES'

Port Sunlight Village (CH62 5DH)

The unlikely but truly historic venue on Saturday 18 August 1962 for the *real* 'Birth of the Beatles'. This marked Ringo Starr's very first appearance as the Beatles' new drummer. The Fab Four were complete. Even Brian Epstein was there to witness the auspicious occasion. It was one of four gigs they were to play in this Tudor-style village hall during 1962 for such hip bodies as the Horticultural Society, the Golf Club and the Recreations Association.

Don't leave this unique and beautiful village, created over a century ago by soap baron Lord Leverhulme, without visiting the 'jewel in the crown', the Lady Lever Art Gallery (inset above). It is truly exquisite and ranks among the world's top art museums. Be prepared to be impressed. Also worth a visit is the Port Sunlight Museum which tells the story of the creation of this model village dating from 1888.

MACDONA HALL *Banks Road/ Salisbury Avenue, West Kirby (CH48 0RD)*

After coming under his wing one week earlier, this was the first real booking the Beatles' new manager Brian Epstein arranged for them. The date was 1 February 1962 and Brian, in true showman style, had advertised it as the 'Grand Opening of 'The Beatle Club'. In fact, this was the only time they played here and nothing more was heard of The Beatle Club. Rendered voiceless with laryngitis, John's place in the band was taken by Ringo's old 'boss' Rory Storm.

The gig took place in the hall used as a dance studio above West 34 restaurant which, in those days, was occupied by the Thistle Café and is now a hairdressing salon.

IRBY VILLAGE HALL

Thingwall Road, Irby
(CH61 3UB)

Another small, tucked away out of sight, village hall played only once by the Beatles when it was home to the Newton Dancing School. This gig took place on 7 September 1962 and was sandwiched between two trips to EMI's Abbey Road Studios, London, to lay down the tracks for their first single – *Love Me Do* and *P.S. I Love You*.

The Irby gig had two notable features. On the cusp of 'the big time', the Beatles' appearance fee was the princely sum of £35. However, the organiser was only able to raise £20 from ticket sales on the night so a jumble sale was later organised to raise the balance. A miffed Brian Epstein turned up in person in his Rolls Royce to collect the outstanding fee.

After the gig, George Harrison had forgotten to take with him his cheap cardboard suitcase with his initials on it together with a small note saying "Mr George Harrison c/o Beatles Party". George never got round to picking it up. Over 40 years later the case was sold to a collector for £5,500. At the same time, a seven shillings (35p) ticket for the dance, together with the letter from Brian confirming the booking, were sold by the dance organiser for the same amount.

BARNSTON WOMEN'S INSTITUTE **Barnston Road, Heswall** (CH60 2UB)

In 1962 the Beatles were booked by the Heswall Jazz Club, which held weekly jazz nights, to play in this village hall. For their first appearance here on Saturday 24 March, no doubt they wore the new Beno Dorn suits they had picked up from Birkenhead just a few weeks earlier. The support band was The Pasadena Jazzmen

On Saturday 30 June, at the second of three gigs they played in this unlikely venue, you could have watched "Parlophone Recording Artistes" the Beatles *and* The Big Three, billed as "One of L'pool's TOP 5 Groups", perform live on stage *and* listen to the top 20 records of the day, all for less than £1. For their final gig here on 25 September that year, Gerry and The Pacemakers provided the support. Tickets for this mid-week event were a very affordable 4/6d (less than 25p).

'REMBRANDT' — PAUL'S FATHER'S HOUSE

Baskervyle Road, Heswall

Overlooking the Dee estuary and the hills of North Wales, this is the house that Paul bought for his father for £8,750 when he returned from America after the Beatles' triumphant tour of America in 1964. Compared with their small terraced house in Forthlin Road, this mock-Tudor detached house was truly palatial.

Crippled by arthritis, Jim McCartney eventually moved to a bungalow nearby and died in March 1976. 'Rembrandt' was bought from his father by Paul and is still owned by him.

Paul wears the distinctive military-type jacket worn by the Beatles at the legendary Shea Stadium concert in New York City on 15 August 1965 when they played to over 55,000 fans amid chaotic scenes of Beatlemania US-style. However, even by the time they made their American debut in 1964, appearing on the Ed Sullivan Show before an estimated 73 million viewers, they were already wealthy young men and Paul was easily able to afford to buy 'Rembrandt' for his father.

Beatles gigs venues

LIVERPOOL CITY CENTRE

Cabaret Club, 28 Duke Street

Cassanova Club
The Temple, Temple Street

*Cassanova Club 1st floor ballroom,
corner London Rd/Fraser Street

*The Cavern Club, 10a Mathew Street
*'Replica' built as part of Cavern Walks
development on same site.*

*David Lewis Theatre, Great George Place

Empire Theatre, Lime Street

*Iron Door Club/Liverpool Jazz Society
13 Temple Street

Jacaranda Coffee Bar, 23 Slater Street

Lewis's Department Store, Ranelagh Street

Liverpool College of Art, Hope Street

Merseyside Civil Service Club, Lower Castle Street

Odd Spot Club, 89 Bold Street

*Odeon Cinema, London Road

Royal Iris Cruiseship, River Mersey.
*Currently lying derelict in the River Thames
at Woolwich. Campaigns to have the vessel
returned to the Mersey and restored have so
far come to nothing.*

ELSEWHERE IN AND AROUND LIVERPOOL

*Aintree Institute, Longmoor Lane

*Albany Cinema, Northway, Maghull

*Blair Hall (Co-op), Walton Road/Christopher Street,
Walton

Casbah Coffee Club, 8 Hayman's Green, West Derby

*Childwall Labour Club

*Bus Depot Social Club, Finch Lane, Nr Huyton

Gateacre Labour Club

Grafton Ballroom, West Derby Road

*Hambleton Hall, St. David's
Road/Princess Drive, Page Moss,
Nr Huyton

Holyoake Hall, Smithdown Road/Blenheim
Road, Nr Penny Lane

Knotty Ash Village Hall
East Prescot Road/Thomas Lane

Lee Park Golf Club, off Childwall Valley Road

Locarno Ballroom, West Derby Road

Lowlands Club, Hayman's Green, West Derby

*Morgue Skiffle Cellar, 25 Oakhill Park, Broadgreen

Mossway Hall, Moss Way, Croxteth

*New Cabaret Artistes, 174a Upper Parliament Street

New Clubmoor Hall (Conservative Club)
Back Broadway

*New Colony Club, 80 Berkley Street

Pavilion Theatre, Lodge Lane

*Picton Road Bus Depot Social Club,
Picton Road, Wavertree

Quarry Bank High School, Harthill Road

*Rialto Ballroom, Upper Parliament Street,
Toxteth

*Rosebery Street, Toxteth

St.Barnabas Church Hall, Penny Lane

St.John's Hall, Snaefell Avenue, Tuebrook

St. Peter's Church Hall, Church Road, Woolton

Stanley Abattoir Social Club, East Prescot Road, Old Swan

Beatles gigs venues

*Starline Club, Windsor Street, Toxteth

Wilson Hall, Speke Road, Garston

*Winter Gardens Ballroom,
Heald Street, Garston

Woolton Village Club, Allerton Road,
Woolton

CROSBY / SEAFORTH / LITHERLAND / BOOTLE

*Alexandra Hall, College Road, Crosby

Lathom Hall, Lathom Avenue, Seaforth

Litherland Town Hall, Hatton Hill Road, Litherland

*St. John's Hall, Oriel Road, Bootle

St. Luke's Hall, Crosby, Church Youth Club

ST HELENS / WIDNES

Town Hall, Earlestown, St Helens

Plaza Ballroom, Duke Street/Crab Street,
St Helens

*Queen's Hall, Widnes

SOUTHPORT

Air Training Corps Club, Upper Aughton Road/Mosley Street,
Birkdale, Nr Southport

Cambridge Hall (now 'The Atkinson'), Lord Street

Floral Hall, Promenade

Glen Park Club, 273 Lord Street

*Kingsway Club, Promenade

Little Theatre, Hoghton Street

*Odeon Cinema, Lord Street

Queens Hotel (now Queen's Hotel Court),
Promenade

Barnston Women's Institute
Barnston Road, Heswall

Ellesmere Port Civic Hall
Whitby Road, Ellesmere Port

Grosvenor Ballroom
Grosvenor Street, Wallasey

Haig Dance Club
Haig Avenue, Moreton

Hulme Hall, Port Sunlight Village

Macdona Hall/Thistle Cafe
Banks Road, West Kirby

Majestic Ballroom
Conway Street, Birkenhead

Neston Institute (now known as Neston Civic Hall)
Hinderton Road, Neston

Irby Village Hall (Newton Dancing School)
Thingwall Road, Irby

*St.Paul's Presbyterian Church Hall
North Road, Tranmere

*Technical College Hall
Borough Road, Birkenhead

*Tower Ballroom
Promenade, New Brighton

YMCA Whetstone Lane,
Birkenhead (replaced by new YMCA building)

*YMCA Birkenhead Road, Hoylake

Victoria Hall
Village Road, Higher Bebington.

Building no longer exists

Beatles gigs venues

13 Pete Best's house & Casbah Club
8 Hayman's Green, West Derby

14 Stu Sutcliffe's house
37 Aigburth Drive, Sefton Park

15 Brian Epstein's house
197 Queen's Drive, Woolton

1 Penny Lane

2 Strawberry Field
Beaconsfield Road, Woolton

3 St Peter's Church, Woolton
John and Paul meet for the first time

4 Mathew Street
Cavern Club/Cavern Quarter

BEATLE COLLEGES

16 John's College of Art
Hope Street

17 Paul and George's college
Liverpool Institute, Mount Street

18 John's college
Quarry Bank Grammar School
Harthill Road, Mossley Hill

BEATLE BIRTHPLACES

5 John's birthplace
Maternity Hospital, Oxford Street

6 Paul's birthplace
Walton Hospital, Rice Lane

7 George's birthplace
12 Arnold Grove, Wavertree

8 Ringo's birthplace
9 Madryn Street, Dingle

OTHER PLACES

19 John, Paul, George and Ringo play together for the first time as the Beatles
Hulme Hall, Port Sunlight Village, Wirral

20 Birthplace of local Beatlemania
Litherland Town Hall

BEATLE HOUSES

9 John's house Mendips,
251 Menlove Avenue, Woolton

10 Paul's house
20 Forthlin Road, Allerton

11 George's house
174 Mackets Lane, Hunts Cross

12 Ringo's house
10 Admiral Grove, Dingle

Penny Lane roundabout

Strawberry Field

1 *Birthplace – Maternity Hospital, Oxford Street*

6 *Liverpool College of Art – Hope Street*

2 *House – Mendips, 251 Menlove Avenue*

7 *John meets Paul for the first time – St Peter's Church Hall*

3 *Strawberry Field – Beaconsfield Road, Woolton*

8 *John marries Cynthia Powell – Mount Pleasant Registry Office*

4 *Infants and Junior School – Dovedale Road, Penny Lane*

9 *First house – 9 Newcastle Road, Penny Lane*

5 *College – Quarry Bank, Harthill Road, Woolton*

10 *Mother's house – 1 Blomfield Road, Allerton*

Top Lennon Sights

1. The Grapes, Mathew Street. The 'go to' pub for the Beatles and other bands performing at the Cavern opposite. Once also a long-time favoured haunt of the Beatles' first manager, Allan Williams, and Cavern DJ Bob Wooler.

2. The White Star. Named after one of the city's most famous shipping companies, this was a handy alternative to The Grapes. Both John's and George's fathers were White Star liner stewards.

3. Ye Cracke, Rice Street. Popular with students from Liverpool College of Art, including John Lennon and Stu Sutcliffe. Art tutorials were sometimes conducted in the back room. John's romance with his first wife Cynthia also began here. In their student days, the pub was smaller; it was later extended and a beer garden added. Seek out the Dissenters plaque.

4. The Philharmonic ('The Phil'), Hope Street. Liverpool's most ornate and famous Victorian pub. John Lennon lamented that the price of fame was "...not being able to go to the Phil for a drink."

5. The Marlborough (now O'Brien's), Slater Street. For those, including the Beatles, who sought an alternative to the Jacaranda's coffee, this was the nearest pub, right next door to the Jac in fact.

6. The Roscoe Arms, Renshaw Street. Next door but one to the former *Merseybeat* newspaper office, this was the obvious choice for the Beatles, other local groups and contributors such as Brian Epstein and Bob Wooler calling to see its editor, Bill Harry.

7. The Cavern Pub, Mathew Street. Not strictly a Beatles pub as it didn't exist during the Merseybeat era, this subterranean pub is worth a visit just to see all the pop memorabilia on display inside and to listen to live music. However, you are likely to dawdle a while before you enter as the bricks on the outside wall display the names of all the hundreds of artists who have performed at the Cavern Club from 1957 to the present day. See if you can spot your favourites. Visitors to the street queue up to have their photo taken with the life-size statue of John Lennon leaning against the wall of the pub.

Three pubs associated with Ringo:

8. The Beaconsfield and **9. The Lisbon**, are Victorian pubs located in the basements of office buildings in Victoria Street, around the corner from Mathew Street. Whilst the Beatles usually waited until after a show before they headed to a pub, Ringo confessed to having a drink in one or other of these pubs not only before a gig but sometimes during the interval as well. His favourite was a 'black and tan' (a mix of Guinness and cider). Apart from enjoying a drink or three, Ringo at that time was a heavy smoker, reputedly puffing his way through three packs a day, ironic considering his lengthy lung-related illness as a youngster. Apart from its decorative pubs and many fine Victorian office buildings, Victoria Street also boasted a subterranean gents toilet which held a particular attraction for gay men, hence its nickname 'the fairy glen'.

10. The Empress, High Park Street, just yards away from Ringo's home in Admiral Grove, features on the cover of his 1970 debut solo album *Sentimental Journey*. Ringo can be seen standing in the pub doorway whilst family members have been montaged into the pub's windows. The album is what it says on the tin; it's a sentimental journey through songs he learnt at his mother's knee during the 1940s and 50s including, of course, *Sentimental Journey*. Whether the Empress could be regarded as Ringo's 'local', however, is debatable According to his close childhood friend, and long-time BeatleGuide Marie Crawford (then Marie McGuire), "It wasn't a young person's pub – Ritchie wouldn't have been seen dead in it and neither would I!"

THE GRAPES

The Grapes is the only traditional pub on Mathew Street. At one time in the early 60's it was in fact the only pub on Mathew Street and was surrounded by warehouses.

Located opposite The Grapes is the Cavern Club. The Beatles would often have a pint here before playing in the club... Inside the pub is a photograph of the Beatles sat in an area preserved with the original seat and wallpaper.

People from all over the world visit the pub to have a drink and be photographed where the Beatles sat.

John Lennon peed here.

Beatles Pubs

THE LIVERPOOL CONNECTION IN 50 PLUS BEATLE SONGS

"You can take the boys out of Liverpool but you can't take Liverpool out of the boys."

From their first tentative efforts as budding songwriters, Lennon and McCartney were inspired by Liverpool, its people and its places. First-time visitors to the city are often surprised to find that there really is a Penny Lane and a Strawberry Field.

Here are songs that had their origins in, or were inspired by, Liverpool, the Beatles' birthplace. The UK album on which it appears is given after each song.

A Day in the Life (*Sgt. Pepper's Lonely Hearts Club Band*)

Part written by John and part by Paul, their contributions were masterfully combined to produce what some would argue is the greatest of the Beatles' songs. Paul wrote the song's middle section, explaining, "It was just me remembering (When he was living in Forthlin Road) what it was like to run up the road to catch a bus to school, having a smoke and going into class...It was a reflection of my schooldays. I would have a woodbine (a 'woodie' was the cheapest cigarette a schoolboy could get his hands on) and somebody would speak and I would go into a dream."

All I've Got To Do (*With The Beatles*)

Written by John in 1961, most probably at Mendips. It was influenced by his love of the Motown sound and in particular Smokey Robinson. John also performed the lead vocals on *Baby It's You* another Motown hit in the same vein in 1961 for the Shirelles.

Cayenne (*Anthology 1*)

A Shadows-style instrumental written by Paul at Forthlin Road when he was about 14, before he met John and not long after he'd got his first guitar, a £15 Framus Zenith.

Do You Want to Know a Secret? (*Please Please Me*)

Written by John after he and Cynthia moved into Brian Epstein's flat at 36 Falkner Street (right) this song has its foundation in another tune his mother sang to him as a young boy. "Want to

know a secret? Promise not to tell?" warbled Snow White in the 1937 Disney classic *Snow White and the Seven Dwarfs*. The actual secret was John's realisation that he really was in love with Cynthia. The song provided Liverpudlian Billy J Kramer with a No. 1 hit in 1963.

John re-wrote the fairytale for his *Spaniard in the Works* book calling it *Snore Wife and the Several Dwarts*.

Eleanor Rigby (*Revolver*)

A number of theories have been put forward to explain the origins of the name Eleanor Rigby. Paul, who wrote the song, thought that 'Eleanor' came from Eleanor Bron the actress who appeared in the Beatles' *Help* whilst 'Rigby' was part of a sign 'Rigby & Evens Ltd', a firm of wine and spirit shippers he

THE LIVERPOOL CONNECTION

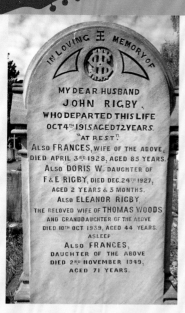

still alive. Paul explained: "We came up with this holiday scenario. I rang up Ringo and said let's pretend that John's gone on holiday and he's sent us a cassette and said, 'Finish it up for me'."

Mainly filmed at various locations around Liverpool, the *Free as a Bird* video is bursting with intriguing references to Beatle songs, including *Penny Lane*, *Strawberry Fields*, *Yellow Submarine* and *Piggies*. Among the many Liverpool locations is the city's most famous building, the Royal Liver Building (below).

had noticed during a visit to Bristol. A more whimsical explanation, which is not possible to confirm is that, perhaps subconsciously, Paul had seen the gravestone of the Eleanor Rigby who is buried in the churchyard of St. Peter's Church, Woolton. The gravestone is just yards away from where Paul had first encountered John.

Paul explained that the Eleanor Rigby character was inspired by his memories of old people he came into contact with whilst running errands as a boy scout.

The video for *Free as a Bird* includes an image of an Eleanor Rigby gravestone, but not *the* gravestone shown above.

Free as a Bird (*Anthology 1*)

Based on a rough demo recorded by John in his New York apartment in 1977, this became the first 'new' Beatles song for 25 years. John's line – "Whatever happened to the boy that I once knew." – fits in with the concept that the song was written for a planned musical about John's life and times in the 60s.

The recording was treated by Paul, George and Ringo as though John was

Glass Onion (*The Beatles – The White Album*)

Written by John to wind up all those fans who tried to outdo each other by finding hidden meanings in Beatle songs (remember the 'Paul is dead' theory?). Apart from Strawberry Fields, another Liverpool placename is mentioned – the cast iron shore or, as we call it, 'The cazzie'. To describe it as a 'beach', however, would be to over-glamourise it. It was, and is, pretty disgusting but as it was the only part of Liverpool's shoreline accessible to the public, it was popular with children from south Liverpool. It takes its name from John Cragg's iron foundry which built two of Liverpool's most famous churches, St. George's, Everton (the world's first cast iron church) and St. Michael's in the Hamlet, Aigburth.

Golden Slumbers (*Abbey Road*)

Conceived by Paul on the piano at the house that he bought his father in Baskervyle Road, Heswall. A song-book belonging to his step-sister Ruth provided the inspiration. It contained the traditional lullaby *Golden Slumbers* by Shakespeare's contemporary, Thomas Dekker. As Paul was unable to read sheet music in those days, he made up his own melody.

Paul: *"We always had a piano. (It's a great-sounding piano, which I still have. It was bought, incidentally, from North End Music Stores, NEMS. Brian Epstein was the son of Harry Epstein, the owner, and my dad bought his first piano from Harry. It is all like that in Liverpool, pretty inter-twined.)".*

"I wrote 'When I'm Sixty-Four' on that when I was still sixteen..."

Good Day Sunshine (*Revolver*)

Written by Paul at John's house on an especially sunny day.

Hello Little Girl (*Anthology 1*)

John's first original song written in late 1957 when he was 17. It was influenced by Buddy Holly's *Maybe Baby* and inspired by a song sung to him by his mother, a Cole Porter number *It's De-lovely* sung by Bob Hope. The song also gave another Liverpool group, The Fourmost, a top ten hit in October 1963. According to Brian O'Hara, the group's leader, John told him he'd written it sitting on the toilet!

Hey Jude (*Past Masters: Vol. 2*)

Written by Paul, it was about John and Cynthia's Liverpool-born five-year old son Julian ('Hey Jules' became *Hey Jude*) with whom Paul had always been close. John said that this was his favourite Paul song.

I Am The Walrus (*Magical Mystery Tour*)

The catalyst for this surreal song was a letter from a pupil at John's old school,
Quarry Bank, explaining that his class had been given the task of analysing the lyrics of Beatle songs. John found this ironic especially as his English teachers had given up on him...Lennon had excelled only in class anarchy. The title was inspired by the poem *The Walrus and The Carpenter* written by John's favourite author, Lewis Carroll. *The Walrus and The Carpenter* was one of ten hand-written and illustrated poems included in John's *My Anthology*, done when he was a 12-year old pupil at Quarry Bank.

The line 'I am the eggman' may have been a reference to another Lewis Carroll character, Humpty Dumpty from *Through The Looking Glass*. Another line 'Yellow matter custard dripping from a dead dog's eye' came from a playground ditty chanted by every Liverpool school-boy in the 40s, and usually directed at more sensitive souls i.e. girls – 'Yellow matter custard, green snot pie, all mixed up with a dead dog's eye. Spread it on a butty, spread it on thick, then wash it down with a cup of cold sick.' Revolting!

The Walrus crops up again on *Glass Onion* ("The Walrus was Paul.") and on the John Lennon/Plastic Ono Band track *God* ("I was the Walrus. But now I'm John").

I Call Your Name (*Past Masters: Vol. 1*)

Although Paul claims to remember working on this song in John's bedroom, John reckoned that he wrote it before he was in the Quarrymen or the Beatles.

I Lost My Little Girl

Influenced by Buddy Holly and perhaps the earliest song written by Paul, it formed part of the Quarrymen's repertoire but was dropped when the group became the Beatles.

I'll Be On My Way (*Live at the BBC*)

Influenced by Buddy Holly, Paul wrote this song in 1961 on his Framus Zenith guitar, probably at Forthlin Road.

I'll Follow The Sun (*Beatles For Sale*)

Another early Paul song composed on his Zenith guitar in the front room of Forthlin Road when he was 16 and recovering from a bout of 'flu. It has been claimed that the inspiration for the song came as he gazed through the lace-curtained front window of his Forthlin Road home.

I'll Get You (*Past Masters: Vol. 1*)

Another song written at 251 Menlove Avenue by John and Paul, the 'B' side of their mega-hit *She Loves You*.

I'm Down (*Past Masters: Vol. 1*)

This frenetic song written by Paul in 1965 pays homage to his, and John's, love of Little Richard who they backed at the Tower Ballroom, New Brighton, three years earlier. During the Beatles' Cavern days, Paul regularly covered Little Richard songs such as *Long Tall Sally* and *Tutti Frutti*. Indeed, Little Richard claimed to have taught his signature 'Wooo!' to Paul during their time together at Hamburg's Star Club – listen to Paul on *I Saw Her Standing There*.

In My Life (*Rubber Soul*)

As the original scribbled lyrics reveal, this song started life as an autobiographical reflection on some of John's favourite Liverpool landmarks as he travelled from Menlove Avenue to the Pier Head. Among the places he remembered were Penny Lane, Church Road (a road that leads from Penny Lane past Newcastle Road where his first home was) and the Clock Tower (Wavertree Clock Tower). "In the circle of the Abbey. I have seen some happy hours.", is a reference to the former Abbey Cinema. "Past the tramsheds with no trams." refers to the Smithdown Road Tram Depot. "On the 5 'bus into town" is the number 5 bus that goes from Woolton, past John's house and on to Liverpool city centre (Liverpudlians have always called their city centre 'town'). "Past the Duchy (a small cafe

and hangout for local teenagers) and St Columba's" (church) "To the dockers umbrella that they pulled down." relates to one of the real wonders of Liverpool and a world-first for the city that was sadly demolished in the 1950s – an overhead electric railway (below) that ran the length of Liverpool docks from Seaforth in the north past the Pier Head finishing at Dingle (near Ringo's home) in the south. Dockers on their way to and from work would shelter under it from the rain.

John's boyhood friend, Pete Shotton, claimed John told him that when he wrote: "...friends I still can recall, some are dead and some are living,.." he was specifically thinking about former Beatle Stu Sutcliffe and Pete.

Up until his death John had always been sentimental about Liverpool and kept a box of momentos in his apartment in the Dakota building in New York. He'd even asked his Aunt MImi to send him his old Quarry Bank school tie.

I Saw Her Standing There (*Please Please Me*)

Conceived by Paul in late 1961, he worked on it at 'Hurricaneville', the home of Rory Storm and his 17-year old sister Iris. She was a professional dancer whom Paul had spotted dancing the twist in her fishnet stockings at the Tower Ballroom, New Brighton. She and Paul dated on and off for a few years. The song was refined by Paul and John in the front room of Paul's house in Forthlin Road (overleaf), the lyrics jotted down in a Liverpool Institute exercise book with Paul starting the ball rolling – "She was just seventeen" and John

The sunny 'front room' of Paul's house at 20 Forthlin Road where much of the magic of the early Lennon and McCartney compositions took place, including 'I Saw Her Standing There' and 'I'll Follow the Sun'.

adding the very Liverpudlian saying – "You know what I mean." It seems highly likely that the song takes its inspiration from one of Paul's Liverpool girlfriends, but which one? Blonde Iris or flame-haired Celia Mortimer, a 17-year art student with whom Paul had hitch-hiked to London and 'danced the night away' at the Establishment Club?

In Spite of All the Danger (*Anthology 1*)

Influenced by Elvis, written by Paul, and with a guitar solo by George, this McCartney/Harrison-attributed number has two claims to fame. It was the embryonic Beatles' first record, made in 1958 in Percy Phillips' small studio at 38 Kensington, Liverpool, for less than £1. Also, it was the only original song performed by the Quarrymen at that time. This historic event is marked by this plaque on the building.

I've Just Seen a Face (*Help!*)

Nicknamed *Aunty Jin's Theme* after Paul's Auntie Jin (Jane Virginia McCartney, Paul's father's youngest sister), this song, written by Paul, was a favourite of hers, sung by him at family get togethers.

Julia (*The Beatles – The White Album*)

Although *Julia* was directed at his mother, John is also telling her that he has found a new love – 'ocean child' (Yoko in Japanese). As Paul said of Julia – "…John absolutely adored her, and not just because she was his mum." Written by John during his latter Beatle days, this gentle song couldn't be more different than *Mother* (see p123)

Lady Madonna (*Past Masters: Vol. 2*)

According to Paul, "Lady Madonna started off as the Virgin Mary, then it was a working-class woman, of which obviously there's millions in Liverpool. There are a lot of Catholics in Liverpool because of the Irish connection." Chiefly written by Paul, perhaps the song was subconciously alluding to his own mother who was also a hardpressed, multi-tasking, working-class Catholic (and working mother) with an Irish ancestry.

Let it Be (*Let It Be*)

The 'Mother Mary' in the opening lines of the song is a reference to Paul's mother providing comfort and guidance from the afterlife.

Like Dreamers Do (*Anthology 1*)

An early Paul number dating from 1959 which became part of the Quarrymen's and then the Beatles' repertoire until 1962.

Love Me Do (*Please Please Me*)

Written jointly by Paul and John in the front room of Forthlin Road whilst sagging off school. John's main contribution was the middle eight and the distinctive harmonica solo. John had played the mouth organ since childhood and had admired Delbert McClinton's harmonica work on Bruce Channel's *Hey Baby*. John was to meet him at the Tower Ballroom in New Brighton a few months before the Beatles recorded *Love Me Do* and Delbert generously showed him his technique. *Love Me Do* is also memorable because producer George Martin wasn't happy with new boy Ringo's drumming and replaced him on the recording with session drummer Andy White.

Maggie Mae (*Let It Be*)

The final 'throw-away' track sung by the Beatles in heavy Scouse accents on the *Let It Be* album, *Maggie Mae* (also *May*) is a well-known Liverpool folk song about a local prostitute who plied her trade in Lime Street and Canning Place (see above right). The song was a hit for the Vipers during the mid-50s skiffle boom and formed part of the Quarrymen's repertoire – John sang it at the Woolton village fete on that fateful afternoon on 6 July 1957 when he and John met for the first time. Julia Lennon

had also played the song at Mendips and John may have learned it from her, most probably on the banjo. It was a song that John was still playing towards the end of his life in New York and Paul included it in the setlist for his Liverpool concert on 1 June 2003.

Liverpool-Welsh playwrite Alun Owen, who's success with the play *No Trams To Lime Street*, led to him writing the screenplay for the Beatles' first film *A Hard Day's Night*, went on to write the musical *Maggie May* with composer Lionel Bart.

Michelle (*Rubber Soul*)

Largely written by Paul, the song had its origins in a party piece with which he amused his, and John's art college, friends. Jan Vaughan, the wife of Ivan Vaughan, who introduced his schoolfriend Paul McCartney to John Lennon, was a French teacher and helped Paul out with the lyrics, coming up with the girl's name – 'Michelle, ma belle' – and the line – 'sont les mots qui vont tres bien ensemble' ('These are words that go together well').

Mother Nature's Son (*The Beatles – The White Album*)

Principally a Paul song, and partly inspired by Nat King Cole's 1947 hit

Nature Boy, it was completed at his father's house in Baskervylle Road, Heswall. A lover of the countryside from the days when he was a boy living in the (in those days) partly-rural Liverpool suburb of Speke, Paul famously 'went back to nature' when he bought an estate on the remote Scottish Mull of Kintyre peninsula in 1966.

Norwegian Wood (*Rubber Soul*)

John said that he wrote this song about an affair he'd had whilst at the same time trying to prevent his wife Cynthia finding out about it. John's friend and fellow Quarryman, Pete Shotton, thought that the song harked back to John's student days in the Gambier Terrace flat (above) he shared with Stu Sutcliffe, specifically the reference to sleeping in the bath and John's practice of burning wooden furniture in the fireplace.

One After 909 (*Let It Be*)

Written by John in 1957, probably in Paul's house at Forthlin Road, although Cynthia recalled helping him with the words in the Jacaranda. Paul elaborated, "We used to sag off school, go back to my house and the two of us would write. There are a lot of songs from back then that we've never reckoned on because they're all very unsophisticated songs...We hated the words to *One After 909*." It was recorded at Percy Phillips' studio but the acetate has not survived.

Penny Lane (*Magical Mystery Tour*)

Although John had first mentioned Penny Lane in the original draft of *In My Life*, it was mainly Paul who wrote this nostalgic song. When Liverpudlians refer to 'Penny Lane' they mean the general area that has the Penny Lane 'roundabout' as its focus. Penny Lane itself is a narrow road that leads from the University of Liverpool's Halls of Residence at Greenbank to its junction with Smithdown Road and Allerton Road. For the first five years of his life John virtually lived in Penny Lane – his home was just around the corner in the family's house at 9 Newcastle Road.

Suburban and mundane though it may appear in real life, Penny Lane is a 'must see' for all Beatle fans visiting Liverpool. The barber's shop is still there although Mr Bioletti, the barber who gave John, Paul and George their 'short back and sides' haircuts when they were children, isn't. One of the three banks that used to be at the 'Penny Lane roundabout' is still here too and so is the 'shelter in the middle of the roundabout', although it's no longer a bus shelter. Further along Allerton Road at its junction with Mather Avenue is the local fire station.

Explaining how the song was written, John said – "It was just reliving childhood." Paul elaborated - "Penny Lane is a bus roundabout in Liverpool; and there is a barber's shop showing photographs of every head he's had the pleasure to know - no that's not true, they're just photos of hairstyles, but all the people who come and go stop and say hello. It's part fact, part nostalgia for a place which is a great place, blue suburban skies as we remember it, and it's still there." Penny Lane takes its name from James Penny, a prominent 18th century Liverpool slave trader.

Please Please Me (*Please Please Me*)

Many of John's musical influences came from his mother Julia and the songs she sang to him as a child. A Bing Crosby hit in the early 30s, *Please* was one such song. A born wordsmith, John was

intrigued with the line – 'Oh please, lend your little ears to my pleas.' and its twin meanings of the words 'please' and 'pleas'. *Please Please Me* was written by John in his bedroom at 251 Menlove Avenue (below). He recalled: "I remember the day and the pink eyelet on the bed." (he probably meant 'coverlet', a bedspread). He'd also been influenced by Roy Orbison's *Only The Lonely* and pictured him singing *Please Please Me* – the original version of John's song was much slower. Written entirely by John.

John's small bedroom at 251 Menlove Avenue where he wrote a number of early Beatles songs.

Polythene Pam (*Abbey Road*)

Written and sung by John – "…I used a thick Liverpool accent because it was supposed to be about a mythical Liverpool scrubber dressed up in her jackboots and kilt."

Supposedly, and unbelievably, a young girl fan of the Beatles called Pat from their Cavern days, had a bizarre habit of eating polythene. She was known to the Beatles as Polythene Pat. Subsequently, John claimed that the song related to an incident when a friend involved him in a threesome with a girl clad in polythene!

PS I Love You (*Please Please Me*)

Mainly written by Paul with some help from John after Paul's girlfriend Dot Rhone visited him in Hamburg. Head over heels in love with Paul, she assumed that he had her in mind when writing this 1962 song, a supposition Paul later denied, explaining that he never had any specific girl in mind. Paul ended their relationship that summer at 93 Garmoyle Road, the flat she shared with John's girlfriend, Cynthia.

Step Inside Love (*Anthology 3*)

The Beatles' association with the Liverpool singer and entertainer Cilla Black went back to the days when she was a cloakroom attendant at the Cavern club. Fitting therefore that Paul should write this as the theme song for her new TV series *Cilla* in 1968. It gave her a top ten hit. She also recorded two other songs – *Love of the Loved*, an old Quarrymen's song that became her first single, and Paul's *It's for You*.

Strawberry Fields Forever (*Magical Mystery Tour*)

John regarded this as his favourite Beatle song. Like Penny Lane, Strawberry Field (no 's' please!) is a real place close to where John lived in Menlove Avenue. In fact he could take a short cut there from his back garden. The wooded grounds of this Salvation Army children's home were familiar to John and his school-friends as they climbed trees and played hide and seek amongst the bushes.

Reputedly, although Paul has denied it, this was the first song on a new album that was to be autobiographical and would develop the Liverpool themes hinted at in songs such as *In My Life* and *Eleanor Rigby*. The idea was abandoned in favour of the Sgt Pepper album and *Strawberry Fields* and *Penny Lane* were issued as a single.

Strawberry Field also gets a mention on *Glass Onion*: "I told you about Strawberry Field. You know the place where nothing is real."

Tell Me What You See (*Help!*)

Written mainly by Paul. John explained that the second verse had its origins in this religious tract that hung on the wall at his home at Mendips:

However black the clouds may be
In time they'll pass away
Have faith and trust and you will see
God's light make bright your day.

We Can Work It Out (*Past Masters 2*)

Written mainly by Paul at his father's house in leafy Heswall on the Wirral. John contributed the middle eight ("Life is very short and there's no time for fussing and fighting my friend")

What Goes On (*Rubber Soul*)

Written by John, "...before the Beatles when we were the Quarrymen or something like that." Paul and Ringo contributed the new middle eight with the latter recording the lead vocals.

When I'm 64 (*Sgt. Pepper's Lonely Hearts Club Band*)

Written in the style of the 20s and 30s songs played by Paul's father in his days heading the Jim Mac Band, it was released when Paul's dad was 64. However, it was composed much earlier on the family piano in Forthlin Road (opposite) when Paul was about 15.

This Yellow Submarine and John Lennon statue were two of the many pieces of 'public art' that featured in Liverpool's International Garden Festival in 1984. Nowadays the Yellow Submarine can be found outside the entrance to Liverpool John Lennon Airport.

Yellow Submarine (*Yellow Submarine*)

The title song of the Beatles' animated film was written by Paul as a children's song to be sung by Ringo. During visits to Merseyside when he had young children of his own, Paul and family would sing *Yellow Submarine* as they travelled under the river through the Mersey Tunnel.

The remixed track and digitally enhanced film were premiered at the Philharmonic Hall, Liverpool, on 14 September 1999.

Yesterday (*Help!*)

Written by Paul in 1964/5, and recorded without any of the other Beatles, it is one of the most covered songs in the history of popular music. Paul has admitted that, subconsciously, he *may* have been alluding to the death of his mother in 1956, just six months after the family had moved into Forthlin Road – "Why she had to go I don't know, she wouldn't say."

You'll Be Mine (*Anthology 1*)

Made in 1960 on a borrowed tape recorder in Paul's house, this knockabout song is noteworthy because it was the very first recording of a Lennon and McCartney number. It may well have been a spoof of an Inkspots song but lead singer John's clowning around also sounds like a send up of The Diamonds' massive 1957 hit *Little Darlin'* – "My darlin' I need you, to call my own...". No doubt like many others in those (for most of us) pre-television days of the 1950s, I wrongly assumed that The Diamonds, like their contemporaries The Searchers, were a black group.

THE SOLO YEARS

The Beatles finally split up in April 1970. In that year each of the Beatles released an album of his own. First out of the stocks was Ringo's *Sentimental Journey* (March) followed by Paul's *McCartney* (April), then George's triple album *All Things Must Pass* (November), although he had released instrumental albums in 1968 and 1969. Finally, in December, John released his *John Lennon/Plastic Ono Band* album.

In their solo recording careers the former members of the Beatles have included many references to their early days in Liverpool. Here are just a few examples.

John

Mother (*John Lennon/Plastic Ono Band, 1970*). The opening song on John's first solo album. The song's gut-wrenching intensity is almost too painful to listen to. Julia was the mother he lost twice – once at the age of five when she handed him over to her sister Mimi to look after and again at the age of 17 when she was killed in a road accident near Mendips, in Menlove Avenue. The song opens with the disquieting sound of a funeral church bell (church bells were rooted in John's childhood – "Sundays, I heard church bells") and ends with John screaming over and over again – "Mummy don't go. Daddy come home".

My Mummy's Dead (*John Lennon/Plastic Ono Band, 1970*). The closing song on John's debut solo album with the death of his beloved mother Julia again as its theme. Pictured above is the grave marker for 'Mummy' (Julia) in Liverpool's Allerton Cemetery.

Working Class Hero (*John Lennon/ Plastic Ono Band 1970*)

John's cynical, world-weary song is firmly grounded in his school and college days in Liverpool. Many people misunderstood the song and thought that John was referring to himself as the working class hero. In fact, John had been brought up in the green and genteel suburb of Woolton in a house that still has the buzzer system with which the master or mistress could summon the domestic help. Although his origins were undeniably working class, John's 'career' since the time he left art college was that of 'musician and artist'.

Ringo

Liverpool 8 (*Liverpool 8, 2008*). Liverpool 8 is the district of Liverpool where Ringo was born and spent all of his formative years until Beatle fame lured him away from his hometown – "Destiny was calling, I just couldn't stick around. Liverpool I left you, but I never let you down." Early jobs, his two Liverpool homes in Madryn Street and Admiral Grove, and his friend Rory of Rory Storm and the Hurricanes, all get mentions. Indeed, Ringo even wrote a song about his old friend: *Rory and the Hurricanes*, the lead song on his 2015 *Postcards From Paradise* album.

In Liverpool (*Ringo 2012*). In this autobiographical song, Ringo tells us about sagging off school to go to Sefton Park, walking to the Iron Door Club and an early job as an apprentice engineer in Liverpool with H. Hunt & Son. But music was in his heart and soul and that's where his destiny lay.

Paul

Early Days (*New 8, 2013*). This is one of three songs on the album where Paul reminisces about his early days in Liverpool, the other two being *On My Way To Work* and *Queenie Eye*. In *Early Days* he sings about how he and John, dressed in black from head to toe walked the streets with guitars on their backs.

That Was Me (*Memory Almost Full, 2007*). His days as a boy scout, playing conkers at the bus stop, the Royal Iris ferry boat and Merseybeat all get an airing on this great number.

INDEX

INDEX

ACKNOWLEDGEMENT

Much of the information in this guide has been gleaned from, or verified by reference to, a number of definitive books about the Beatles written over the years by my friend Mark Lewisohn. *The Complete Beatles Chronicle* and his masterly book about the early years of the Beatles, *The Beatles – All These Years: Tune In* (Published by Little, Brown, London, 2013. ISBN 978-0316-72960-4) have been particularly useful. The latter book tells the story of the Beatles, individually and collectively, until the end of 1962, essentially their Liverpool years. By then, although they were still playing the Cavern and other local venues, they had made their first EMI recordings with George Martin at Abbey Road Studios.

Mark has spent the greater part of his life researching the Beatles of whom he is unquestionably *the* world authority. His books are based on what can only be described as forensic research. If you are interested in discovering the full and truly fascinating story of how four 'ordinary' lads from Liverpool became a worldwide phenomenon, *The Beatles – All These Years: Tune In* is essential reading. And there is more to come; he is currently working on two more volumes to complete the Beatles' story.

However, the production of this book has been almost entirely a solo effort, even down to design, artwork and proofreading. I therefore take sole responsibility for any errors or ommissions of which, inevitably, there will be some!

IMAGE CREDITS

Pete Best – 83 (centre)
The late Bill Connell (Peter Kaye) – 3, 19 (bottom), 27 (inset), 43 (right), 48, 49 (bottom right), 55 (top), 59, 88 (circled), 107 (bottom), 108 (bottom).
National Museums Liverpool (Walker Art Gallery) – 17 (top)
Ann Mason – 33 (top right)
Getty Images – 42, 94-95
John Mills/Liverpool City Council – 49 (top left and centre)
The late Maurice Cockrill R.A. – 121 (top)
EMI Records Ltd – 72
Leslie Kearney – 109 (top)
Liverpool Echo – 14, (top right)

The former Mersey Partnership – Visitor Map, inside back cover.
National Trust – 72 (bottom), 73 (top right), 82, 83, 118 (top). *These digital images are the property of NTPL and are protected by copyright.*
Geoff Rhind – 76-77, 108 (top)
The late Graham Spencer – 98 (top)
Don Valentine – 102

With the exception of a small number of photographs whose ownership is not known to me (I would be pleased to give due acknowledgement in future editions), all other images were taken by the author or are from his personal collection of historic images.

LIVERPOOL

Birthplace of the Beatles